Chicago
CURIOSITIES

Help Us Keep This Guide Up to Date

Every effort has been made by the author and editors to make this guide as accurate and useful as possible. However, many things can change after a guide is published— establishments close, phone numbers change, hiking trails are rerouted, facilities come under new management, etc.

We would love to hear from you concerning your experiences with this guide and how you feel it could be made better and be kept up to date. While we may not be able to respond to all comments and suggestions, we'll take them to heart and we'll also make certain to share them with the author. Please send your comments and suggestions to the following address:

The Globe Pequot Press
Reader Response/Editorial Department
P.O. Box 480
Guilford, CT 06437

Or you may e-mail us at:
editorial@GlobePequot.com

Thanks for your input, and happy travels!

Curiosities Series

Chicago
CURIOSITIES

Quirky characters,
roadside oddities &
other offbeat stuff

Scotti Cohn

Guilford, Connecticut
Helena, Montana
An imprint of Rowman & Littlefield

The prices, rates, and hours listed in this guidebook were confirmed at press time. We recommend, however, that you call establishments to obtain current information before traveling.

For all my Chicago Peeps:
You know who you are!

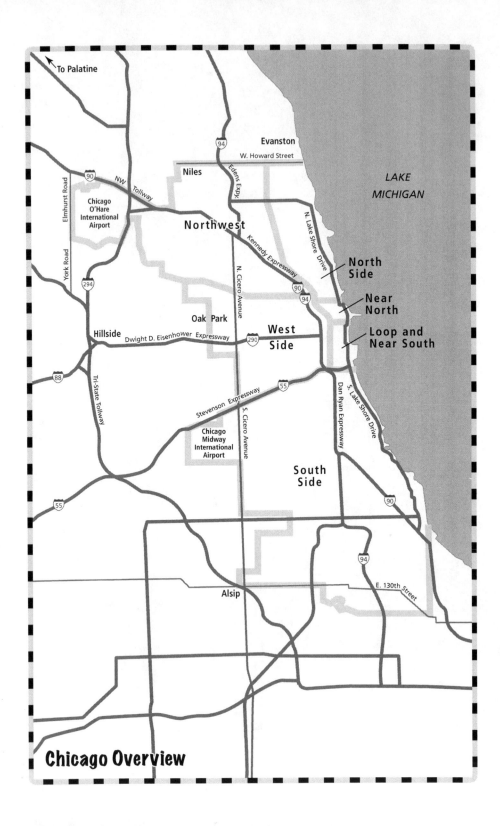

Chicago Overview

contents

acknowledgments

*F*irst, I want to thank my editors at Globe Pequot Press, Erin Turner, Meredith Rufino, and John Burbidge, as well as the rest of the folks at Globe who helped take this book from idea to final product.

I am also grateful to the following people for their assistance, support, and encouragement in the creation of this book: Doug Ahlgrim, Rachel Baker, Phil Barber, Reggie Brown, Susie Daly, Jeffrey Fauver, Dustin Gold, Abbey Hambright, Jane Hertenstein, Ric Hess, Susan Hooper, JoJo Baby, Vicki Matranga, Greg Mele, Paula Morrow, Sandro Mussa-Ivaldi, Terry Pfister, Sandy Ramsey, Kim Schaller, Denise Schneider, Steve Scott, and Philip Wille. Last (and most), I thank my husband, Ray—for everything.

introduction

*A*s the author of *It Happened in Chicago* (Globe Pequot Press, 2009), which focuses on events that occurred over the city's history, I knew I would enjoy working on a book that focuses on "curiosities" that can be seen and experienced in modern-day Chicago.

The most challenging thing about putting this book together was deciding how to organize the curiosities I discovered by geographical section. The Social Science Research Committee at the University of Chicago has divided Chicago into seventy-seven well-defined community areas. But the average Chicagoan doesn't refer to his neighborhood as, for example, "Community Area Number 55."

Typically, Chicagoans use terms such as Loop, Near North Side, West Side, South Side, and so forth. The names and boundaries of these neighborhoods shift and change, depending on who is describing them. There are those who will disagree with the placement of some of my curiosities, but on the whole, I think I've done a pretty good job.

My purpose in writing this book is to celebrate a city that bubbles over with wonderfully quirky people, places, and phenomena. I hope you enjoy these curiosities, whether they make you chuckle, marvel, giggle, or groan.

1

Loop and Near South

The Loop is *Chicago's business district, named after the looping route of streetcars that once served the city. Elevated trains now encircle the downtown area along roughly the same path. The Loop is where business meets pleasure in the form of art, recreation, and culture.*

The Loop contains such famous structures and institutions as the Monadnock Building, the Chicago Cultural Center (formerly Chicago's oldest public library), the Art Institute of Chicago, and the Civic Opera House. If you're interested in a night at the theater, you can choose from the best, including the Goodman, Chicago, Auditorium, Cadillac Palace, Bank of America (Shubert Theatre) and the Ford Center for the Performing Arts (Oriental Theatre).

Grant Park, often referred to as "Chicago's Front Yard," is part of the Loop. Millennium Park, which officially opened in 2004, offers some of the most fascinating and "curious" sculptures in the world.

The Near South Side has changed dramatically over the years. At the time of the Great Fire of 1871, Prairie Avenue was the city's most prestigious street. Printer's Row, once the home of Chicago's printing and publishing industry, is now a residential area. A stroll through the old Dearborn Station will take you back to the heyday of travel by rail.

The Near South Side is known for its world-class natural science museums: the Field Museum of Natural History, the Shedd Aquarium, and the Adler Planetarium. Here you'll also find Soldier Field, home of the Chicago Bears professional football team.

Come Fly with Me!

Savings of America Mural

So you're walking past 120 North LaSalle St. when something catches your eye. There are wings involved, along with huge swatches of blue and white, and a couple of guys in short white tunics.

No, you haven't stumbled onto the annual Chicago Greek Parade. What you've encountered is a mural that arches over the entrance of

Looks like fun, but things didn't turn out so well for Icarus . . .

★ ★

the Savings of America building. If you don't know Greek mythology, there's no telling what you're going to make of this mural.

If you do know Greek mythology, you might realize that the two winged fellows are Daedalus and Icarus. Daedalus, an architect, inventor, and master craftsman, made a pair of artificial wings for himself and his son, Icarus. Daedalus warned his son not to fly too close to the sun, but Icarus got careless. The sun melted the wax holding his wings together, and he fell into the sea and drowned.

Created by artist Roger Brown, *The Flight of Daedalus and Icarus* is rendered in Italian glass mosaic. Brown, who died in 1997, was known for incorporating wry commentary into his works of art. Placed on the Savings of America building, the image of Daedalus and Icarus may well carry a message for the leaders of industry.

It's Right There in Black and White!
Monument with Standing Beast

My initial reaction to Jean Dubuffet's white fiberglass sculpture *Monument with Standing Beast* was that I wished it had been in my backyard or a nearby park when I was growing up. Dubuffet described the sculpture as a "drawing which extends . . . into space." He wanted it to be something people could experience, rather than just a structure to be simply viewed.

Unveiled in 1984, the sculpture is formed of four interrelated elements that are said to represent a standing animal, a tree, a portal, and an architectural form. To me it looks sort of like an ice castle where the Snow Queen would live, or a huge piece of crumpled paper which, when unfolded, might become something glorious before crunching itself back up and freezing in place.

At 29 feet tall, the sculpture is dwarfed by the seventeen-story James R. Thompson Center, on whose plaza it sits. Yet *Monument with Standing Beast* holds its own, catching your eye, drawing you to its side. You can see it at 100 West Randolph St.

Jean Dubuffet's white fiberglass
sculpture invites visitors to enter it.

★ ★

Alas, Poor Del!
The Skull at the Goodman Theatre

You may not have heard of Del Close, but what about Bill Murray, Joan Rivers, John Candy, or Tina Fey? Del Close had a significant influence on all of them. An actor and improvisational comic, Del played mentor and guru to a startling number of the twentieth century's most prominent comedians.

According to Del's friend Kim "Howard" Johnson, the comic's deathbed scene in 1999 was worthy of an award. As jazz musicians, nurses, reporters, friends, and cameramen gathered around, Del declared that he wanted to bequeath his skull to the Goodman Theatre. He imagined the theater might use it in a production of *Hamlet,* for the scene in which the Danish prince unearths a skull and declares, "Alas, poor Yorick!"

A dying man's last wish (or a reasonable facsimile thereof)

The hospital refused to honor Del's wishes. Undaunted, Del's partner, Charna, purchased a skull from a medical supply company, and she and her sister pulled out as many teeth as they could in order to make it resemble Del more . . . um . . . Closely. The ersatz "skull of Del Close" now resides in the associate producer's office at the Goodman on a red velvet cushion in a Lucite case.

The Goodman Theatre is located at 170 North Dearborn St.

Advertising a Work of Art
The Oliver Typewriter Building

In these days of loud and blatant advertising, one longs for the times when promotion was more subtle and artistic. Take, for example, the Oliver Building on North Dearborn Street. Designed by the architectural firm of Holabird & Roche, it was built in 1907, with two more floors being added in 1920, for a total of seven stories.

The facade of the building is striking, with its dark green cast-iron ornamentation of rams, lions, and fish. When gazing at the delicate ironwork, one's subconscious may or may not register the fact that the company's name appears on the building in no fewer than

Trivia

In 2003, in the dead of night, crews under orders from mayor Richard J. Daley bulldozed large gouges into the runway surface at Meigs Field, an airport located on Northerly Island, a peninsula that juts into Lake Michigan. The Federal Aviation Administration was not notified in advance, nor were airplane owners. The mayor wanted the airport closed, and closed it was, leaving sixteen planes stranded.

twenty-six places. A less obtrusive rendering of "The Oliver Typewriter Company" can scarcely be imagined.

The Oliver Building is at 159 North Dearborn St. It was designated a Chicago Landmark in 1984.

Going Up?
The Sky Chapel

If you want to visit the Sky Chapel, you'll need to go up. Way up. Like two elevators and a set of stairs "up." Located in the Chicago Temple Building, the chapel sits 400 feet above the streets of the Windy City.

The Temple Building, a neo-Gothic-style skyscraper designed by Holabird & Roche for the First United Methodist Church, was completed in 1924. It has twenty-three floors devoted to religious and office use (legendary attorney Clarence Darrow once had an office on the sixth floor). The Sky Chapel, installed in 1952, was a gift from Myrtle Walgreen in honor of her husband, who founded the Walgreen's drugstore chain. Seating only about thirty people, it is used primarily for gatherings such as baptisms, weddings, and funerals.

At 568 feet tall, the Chicago Temple Building is the tallest church building in the world, although not the tallest church in the world. That honor belongs to the Ulm cathedral in Ulm, Germany. The First United Methodist Church, founded in 1831, is the oldest church congregation in Chicago.

The Chicago Temple Building is located at 77 West Washington St. For more information, call (312) 236-4548 or visit www.chicago temple.org.

A Baboon/Horse/Grasshopper by Any Other Name
The Picasso

As the story goes, when artist Pablo Picasso was eighty-two years old, an architectural firm approached him about creating a sculpture that would stand outside the Chicago Civic Center (now the Richard J.

Daley Center). Supposedly, Picasso was offered $100,000 but turned down the money, stating that the sculpture would be his gift to Chicago.

The completed work of art, constructed of the same type of steel as that used for the Civic Center, is 50 feet tall and weighs 162 tons.

The Name Game

More than 300 years after explorers Louis Jolliet and Father Jacques Marquette set foot in the area, scholars, linguists, and etymologists are still debating the origin and meaning of the name "Chicago." Everyone seems to agree that the name came from a Native American word. But which word? And what was the correct meaning of that word? Researcher John F. Swenson presents a convincing argument that "Chicago" refers to a wild garlic or leek plant and was likely a reference to a large patch of this plant, which would have been useful as a survival food.

Contrary to popular belief, Chicago's most common nickname, "the Windy City," probably did not originate in 1890 with Charles Dana, editor of the *New York Sun*. For one thing, his words have never been found; it can't be proven that he ever wrote them. For another thing, the nickname appears as early as 1860 in a Milwaukee newspaper. Ohio newspapers also used the term repeatedly during the 1870s— meaning "windy" both literally and figuratively (as a reference to bragging).

Poet Carl Sandburg is responsible for a couple of other popular Chicago nicknames: "City of the Big Shoulders" and "Hog Butcher for the World."

It was unveiled in 1967 by Mayor Daley, who declared: "What is strange to us today will be familiar tomorrow."

Strange indeed. The sculpture has been said to resemble, variously, a woman's head, an Afghan hound, a rusty tin can, a baboon with wings, a predatory grasshopper, a horse, an angel, a cow sticking out its tongue, a human rib cage and appendix, and a Viking ship. Me? I think it looks an awful lot like Big Bird.

One day not too long ago, I noticed that the Picasso was wearing a Chicago Blackhawks hockey helmet. The Blackhawks had made it into the 2010 Stanley Cup Playoffs. In Chicago, even the sculptures are sports fans.

The Chicago Picasso, featured on the cover of *Chicago Curiosities,* is located at 50 West Washington St.

Does Anybody Really Know What Time It Is?
The Great Clocks

Decades before Robert Lamm of the rock band Chicago wrote the song referenced in the title of this entry, Chicago merchant Marshall Field was making a special effort to let everybody know what time it was.

In 1897 the first of the Great Clocks was installed over the entrance of the twelve-story granite building housing Marshall Field and Company. Mr. Field liked the idea of his store being a meeting place, and the clock—designed by Pierce Anderson—could be seen for miles. That same year, Field erected a second Great Clock on another corner of the building.

To this day, people often arrange to meet under one of the clocks, each of which weighs about seven and a half tons. Sometimes the timepieces are "dressed up" to reflect city or store events. For example, they wear chef's hats during Culinary Week.

The Great Clocks, located at 111 North State St., were equipped with GPS (Global Positioning System) technology in 2009 to ensure that everybody really does know what time it is.

Thanks to Marshall Field, everybody on
State Street knows what time it is!

★ ★

Smurfette in the Sky with Diamonds?

The Smurfit-Stone Building

I confess that at first, I wanted to include the Smurfit-Stone Building in this book simply because of its name. I know it's silly, but I pictured myself going into this building and seeing Papa Smurf, Smurfette,

The Smurfit-Stone Building

Brainy Smurf . . . well, you get the idea. I just wasn't sure that the name alone was "curious" enough. Then I found out about the whole feng shui thing.

You see, the most noticeable feature of the Smurfit-Stone Building is its sharply slanted, diamond-shaped roof (it's actually two almost identical triangles with their edges nearly touching). Feng shui experts declared that this was "bad feng shui" for the city. According to feng shui principles, odd shapes direct energy in uneven or chaotic ways. On the Smurfit-Stone Building, the sharp tip of the diamond is like an arrow pointing directly at people and buildings below.

As it turned out, bad feng shui wasn't the only problem. Ice had a nasty habit of sliding off the sloping roof, injuring people coming into the building. The entrance had to be moved to the other side to reduce the probability.

But there is still the matter of that sharp point aimed at innocent passersby. Can Papa Smurf find a way to remedy this bad feng shui? Tune in next week!

The Smurfit-Stone Building is located at 150 North Michigan Ave.

Trivia

When the Sun-Times Building at 401 North Wabash was demolished in 2004, a time capsule designed to last 18,000 years was uncovered. This would have been exciting except for the fact that the capsule was less than fifty years old. It had been placed in 1958 when the structure was built.

★ ★

Cool Bean!
Cloud Gate

The name *Cloud Gate* may sound like it refers to a scandal involving the National Weather Service. In fact, it refers to a 66-foot long, 33-foot high, 42-foot wide, 110-ton sculpture inspired by a drop of liquid mercury, which it strongly resembles.

Stay with me here. This is Chicago. Anything is possible.

In creating *Cloud Gate,* sculptor Anish Kapoor wanted to "make something that would engage the Chicago skyline . . . so that one will see the clouds kind of floating in, with those very tall buildings reflected in the work." He succeeded (brilliantly, I might add). Eighty percent of the stainless steel sculpture's surface reflects the sky.

Not everyone was impressed when the partially completed sculpture was unveiled in 2004. Some called it unimaginative. Others labeled it "The Electric Kidney Bean." Ultimately, Mr. Bean . . . er . . .

Inspired by liquid mercury, "The Bean" dazzles and delights.

Mr. Kapoor had the last laugh on his detractors. The semifinished sculpture became such a public favorite that completion had to be postponed. Massive crowds gathered in Millennium Park to interact with *Cloud Gate*, aka "The Bean." In April 2006 the buffed, polished, final product was revealed, and it continues to draw large crowds.

The "gate" part of *Cloud Gate* is a 12-foot-tall arch under which visitors can walk, stand, sit, or lie on the ground, gazing at reflections in the polished surface. The chamber created by the arch is like a hall of mirrors. You are surrounded, enveloped, transported to another realm or maybe a parallel universe in which everything seems vaguely familiar yet wonderfully strange. It's futuristic, magical, magnificent, mind-bending, elegant, ever-changing, and irresistible. Those who call it "unimaginative" are perhaps, well, a bit unimaginative themselves.

Cloud Gate is located in Millennium Park, which is bounded by Michigan Avenue on the west, Columbus Drive on the east, Randolph Street on the north, and Monroe Street on the south. For more information, call (312) 742-1168 or visit www.millenniumpark.org.

How to Turn Spouting and Spitting into an Art Form
The Crown Fountain

If your attitude about fountains is something like "ya seen one, ya seen 'em all," you may want to prepare for an adjustment. The Crown Fountain in Millennium Park puts a whole new face on the spouting and spewing of streams of water.

The Crown Fountain was designed by Spanish artist Jaume Plensa and named in honor of the Lester Crown family. Completed in 2004, the fountain features two 50-foot towers made of glass blocks, facing each other across a shallow pool. The towers are 23 feet wide and 50 feet high, nearly twice as tall as the average movie screen. Behind the glass blocks are LED screens that randomly display a person's face, a nature scene, or a solid color. Water continuously falls from the sides and back of each tower.

It's the person's face you want to keep an eye on. Periodically, a

Nance Klehm: Urban Weedeater

When Nance Klehm says she's going to pick up lamb's-quarter for dinner, she doesn't mean she'll swing by the supermarket for a leg of mutton. Instead, she'll walk or bike Chicago's highways and byways, pruning shears in hand, eyes searching for *Chenopodium album*—or lamb's-quarter—a tall plant related to spinach, Swiss chard, and beets.

What Klehm does is called urban foraging. In addition to lamb's-quarter, she harvests wood sorrel, mallow, chickweed, chicory greens, watercress, burdock, dandelions—and various other flora, all of which grow, unbidden, in or near the city's parks, sidewalks, train tracks, and parking lots.

Klehm has been foraging for medicinal and edible plants in Chicago for several years. A few times a year she offers guided foraging expeditions and cooking workshops, during which she points out the health and environmental benefits of eating a more natural diet. Among many other activities, she writes a regular column for *Arthur Magazine* called "Weedeater." (You have to love that name.)

Klehm's lifestyle is unusual from another standpoint as well: She's a firm believer in ecological sanitation—composting one's waste instead of flushing it down a toilet. "Stop sewage spills by composting your crap," she writes in her blog. "It's fun. Joyful. Sensible."

For more information about Nance Klehm and her projects, visit http://spontaneousvegetation.net or http://humblepilechicago.blogspot.com.

The Crown Fountain features "spitting
images" of hundreds of Chicagoans.

6-inch nozzle shoots water out of the person's mouth. Many Chicagoans look for their own face on the towers. More than 800 posed for the pictures that were used during the first two years of the fountain's life, and the original plans included updating the images from year to year.

Writing for the *Chicago Tribune* in 2007, Ellen Fox commented that Chicagoans had lovingly retitled the fountain "The Big Videos of the Faces that Spit Water Sometimes and the Kids All Run Around In It." I can't improve on that description.

The Crown Fountain anchors the southwest corner of Millennium Park at Michigan Avenue and Monroe Street. For more information, call (312) 742-1168 or visit www.millenniumpark.org/artand architecture/crown_fountain.html.

★ ★

Felines Who Dress for Success
The Art Institute Lions

Statistics show that lions can live to be thirty years old in captivity. Bronze lions can live even longer, as proved by the two who guard the entrance to the Art Institute of Chicago. They've been there since 1894, the year after the building itself was erected.

Are *you* going to tell him he's a sissy for wearing a bow?
ANDY SPENCER

People often wonder if the lions have names. I have only ever heard them called "north lion" and "south lion." If you think they're identical, look again. The sculptor, Edward Kemeys, gave them similar yet different poses. One is "on the prowl" and the other "stands in an attitude of defiance."

The lions are larger than life, but not fearsome enough to discourage the Art Institute staff from decorating them at will. For example, you can always tell when the Chicago Bears are winning because the lions will be wearing Bears helmets. At Christmas, huge wreaths are placed over the big cats' necks, making them about as festive as lions can possibly be.

The north and south lions (and the Art Institute) are located at 111 South Michigan Ave. (Michigan Avenue at Adams Street).

Dead Drunk?

On July 17, 1869, a man called "Express" Smith was involved in a terrible accident in the Washington Street Tunnel when his wagon crashed into a wall. Smith's companion was quickly revived, but Smith did not move. As he appeared to be dead, his body was transported to the police station, and the coroner was summoned.

Meanwhile, for reasons unexplained, several policemen carried Smith to a sink and poured water on his head. Smith's leg twitched. His arms flailed. He opened his eyes! "Gorry, haven't I been drunk, though?" he exclaimed. The coroner and undertaker were notified of a change in plans.

★ ★

The Alley That Time Forgot

Pickwick Lane

Imagine that you have traveled back in time to the 1860s. You are surrounded by farmland, standing on a spot that will one day become East Jackson Boulevard in Chicago. As you face north, you see a stable, two stories high. You smell hay and hear a horse whinny. A man comes around the corner of the building. He is Henry Horner, grocer and flour merchant, owner of the stable, and grandfather of a future governor of Illinois.

You stay rooted to the spot as time fast-forwards in a blur. Now you inhale the aroma of meat cooking. It's 1899 and you're standing on a narrow cobblestone street called Pickwick Place that leads to Abson's English Chop House. The sounds of voices and clinking glasses drift toward you.

The El rumbles overhead and you lose your bearings for a moment. When you come back to your senses, you're staring at the Red Path Inn. It's 1934. A radio blares from an open window, and an excited announcer declares that "Public Enemy No. 1" John Dillinger has just been shot by FBI agents outside the Biograph Theater on North Lincoln Avenue.

Again time sweeps over you in waves. The name on the building changes from Red Path Inn to Robinson's to Pickwick Cafe. As your mind clears, you see that the same little brick structure is now wedged between towering office buildings. A third story has been added. The same cobblestone path, just 9 feet wide, leads to the entrance.

Inside is a restaurant called 22 East. You walk through a dark, quiet bar on the ground floor and climb a winding staircase to a tiny dining room. "We've been here five years," a woman named Freda tells you. "Since 1942." It's so quiet in this place, it could be a library reading room. Freda and her daughter, Mitzi, describe the day's offerings: chicken liver with apple fritters and french-fried shrimp.

Before you can place your order, the wheel of time turns again,

Pickwick Lane: a window into the past

and you are transported to the twenty-first century. The noise nearly knocks you down. Horns honk, brakes screech, the El thunders, a jackhammer seems to be drilling directly into your ear. Pickwick Lane's cobblestones are gone, replaced by concrete. What is this tiny alley? you wonder. Why would anyone even notice it? As you turn to leave, you're almost certain you hear the faint whinny of a horse.

Pickwick Lane is located at 22 East Jackson Blvd., bounded by Jackson, Wabash Avenue, Adams Street, and State Street.

★ ★

Prost!

The Berghoff

In the beginning, it was all about the beer. Or perhaps I should say *das Bier*. Herman Joseph Berghoff came to America in 1870 from Dortmund, Germany. He and his three brothers brewed beer in Fort

The Berghoff: In the beginning, it was all about the beer.

Wayne, Indiana, for more than twenty years. By then Berghoff was ready to expand his business, and Chicago's World's Columbian Exposition of 1893 gave him the perfect opportunity.

Fairgoers loved his Dortmunder-style beer, and in 1898 Berghoff opened a bar at the corner of State and Adams Streets. Critics gave him six months. He gave the critics absolutely no credence and proceeded to create a Chicago institution.

Now located at 17 West Adams St., Berghoff Catering & Restaurant Group is housed on four floors behind a historical facade that hasn't changed since 1950. Over the years the interior has been enhanced and the menu has been expanded, but Berghoff's descendants continue to preserve his century-old ideals.

Legendary for its creamed spinach and apple strudel, the Berghoff still serves its trademark full-bodied beer, as well as the exceptionally rich-tasting Berghoff Root Beer, created during Prohibition. For more information, call (312) 427-3170 or visit www.theberghoff.com.

Terrifying Bug or Pretty Bird?
Flamingo

In black and white, Alexander Calder's *Flamingo* sculpture looks kind of like the main character from the movie *Deadly Mantis*. I can imagine one of those long legs reaching through a window in the Kluczynski Federal Building and . . . (shudder) I can't go on!

In color, the sculpture is bright vermillion. The exact shade has come to be called "Calder red." It was chosen to offset *Flamingo* from the black and steel edifices that surround it at Federal Center Plaza. *Flamingo*'s arches and curves also contrast dramatically with the angular appearance of the buildings.

Calder had a way of using huge, heavy pieces to create a strangely delicate-looking work of art reminiscent of a mobile. When I look at this sculpture in color, I am able to imagine a lovely, graceful flamingo (yes, I know flamingos aren't typically 53 feet tall). I feel relaxed and calm. A flamingo would never devour Chicago, would it?

Flamingo is located at the intersection of Adams and Dearborn Streets.

Alexander Calder's *Flamingo* looks like it's wading across Federal Center Plaza.

★ ★

Trivia

Historic Route 66 begins in Chicago at Grant Park on Adams Street in front of the Art Institute of Chicago.

And . . . It's Bigger than a Bread Box

The Monadnock Building

It's time for a multiple-choice quiz. Monadnock is (a) a mountain in New Hampshire, (b) a Union navy ship, (c) an isolated hill or a lone mountain that has risen above the surrounding area, (d) a building in Chicago, (e) bigger than a bread box, (f) all of the above.

The answer is (f). The word *monadnock* is thought to derive from the Abenaki Indian language; the meaning is seen in choice (c) above. The building in Chicago—choice (d)—was originally owned by a family from New England, who got its name from Mount Monadnock in New Hampshire—choice (a). At one time, each of the four entrances was named for a different mountain in that region. There have been several ships called USS *Monadnock,* including one launched in 1863 for the Union cause—choice (b).

Another curious thing about the Monadnock Building is that its two halves were built by different architects, in different styles. The northern portion is ultramodern, with no exterior ornamentation. The southern half showcases classical architectural principles.

The Monadnock Building is located at 53 West Jackson Blvd. It's bounded by Jackson Boulevard and Dearborn, Federal, and Van Buren Streets. For more information, visit www.monadnockbuilding.com.

★ ★

The Dynamic Trio?

The Board of Trade Building

No doubt about it, the forty-five-story Board of Trade Building is majestic. So majestic, in fact, that it played the role of the headquarters of Wayne Enterprises in the movie *Batman Begins.* If you look way up high, above the clock centered on the side of the building facing north, you'll see a winged creature who could very well be a bat! However, it's an eagle. (Sorry, you can't have everything.)

And the answer is: an Egyptian, an eagle, and a Native American.

There are two human figures on either side of the eagle. No, they are not Batman and Robin. One is a hooded figure, said to be an Egyptian holding grain. The other is a Native American holding corn. I know, it sounds like a premise for a joke: "An Egyptian, an eagle, and a Native American walk into a bar . . ."

Lovers of artwork and sculpture can have a field day wandering around and through this building, which was designed by architects Holabird & Root. Topping it all off (literally) is a 31-foot-tall aluminum statue of the Roman goddess of grain. The sculptor left the statue's face blank because he was pretty sure no one would ever get close enough to see it. (I can't confirm that because I'm one of those people who can't get close enough to see it.)

The Board of Trade Building is located at 141 West Jackson Blvd.

Want to Stand Out?
Willis Tower Ledge

The Ledge at Skydeck Chicago is attached to the 103rd floor of the 110-story Willis Tower (formerly the Sears Tower). This architectural wonder consists of a series of fully enclosed balconies made of half-inch-thick clear, tempered, laminated glass. The boxes retract into the building to allow easy access for maintenance.

As a tourist attraction, the Ledge is a standout. Literally. Here's how you can experience it:

1. Enter Willis Tower.
2. Take the elevator up, up, up to the 103rd floor.
3. Step out into a glass box that extends 4.3 feet off the Skydeck. (By "glass box" I mean there's glass above, around, and beneath you.)
4. Realize that you are now looking at Chicago—and possibly Michigan, Indiana, and Wisconsin—in a whole new way. On a clear day, you can see 40 to 50 miles, or 65 to 80 kilometers.

To get that "on top of the world" feeling, just step out onto the Ledge!
STEVEN EPSTEIN

5. At this point you can (a) freeze in terror, (b) faint, (c) admire the view, (d) take pictures, (e) do a handstand, or (f) all of the above.

Have you ever had one of those dreams where you're flying above a large city? That's what the view from the Ledge reminds me of.

Willis Tower is located at 233 South Wacker Dr. Enter the Skydeck on Jackson Boulevard (south side of the building). For more information about the Ledge, call (312) 875-9696 or visit www.theskydeck .com/theledge.asp.

Presidential Backup Plan?
Obama's Hair Design

When I saw the sign in the window on South Dearborn Street, I wondered if Barack and Michelle had a little side business going, or maybe they had a backup plan in case the whole presidential thing didn't work out. I also wondered if Obama had relatives in Chicago. A quick Internet search revealed the truth, and voilà! I had another "Chicago curiosity."

According to newspaper reports, the salon used to be called Ossama's. That was a nice enough name before September 11, 2001.

What's in a name? Plenty!

He Reminds Me of Someone . . .

In 2004 Chicago native Reggie Brown's brother Lawrence told him about a guy he had seen working out at the East Bank Club, a guy who looked enough like Reggie to be his twin. A few months later, a customer at a restaurant where Brown worked said he looked like a professor she had known at the University of Chicago.

Intrigued, Brown searched the Internet, where he found a photo of the professor, now a state senator. The state senator then became a U.S. senator. Brown, a model and actor, started to notice people staring at him on the street. He was pretty sure it wasn't because of his voiceover work or his role as an emcee at fashion events.

By 2008 Brown was being told fairly often that he strongly resembled the senator from Illinois. The next year, Reggie Brown's look-alike became America's forty-fourth president.

Brown's efforts to find work as a Barack Obama impersonator picked up considerably after he posted a video of himself holding a mock press conference on YouTube. He was even cast as President Obama in a movie. He now travels the world impersonating Obama.

For more information about Reggie Brown—whose official bio describes him as "that other tall, skinny guy from Chicago"—visit www.reggiebrownasobama.com.

This may not be who you think it is . . .
© 2010 REGGIE BROWN, DUSTIN GOLD, AND BARBERGOLD MANAGEMENT

After that, not so much. Business fell off dramatically.

During the 2009 presidential campaign, the new owner, Mike Elsheikh, thought a new name for the salon was in order. He had met Barack Obama a few years earlier when they both lived in Hyde Park, and he was pretty sure Obama was going to win the election. Ossama's or Obama's? Talk about a no-brainer!

Obama's Hair Design is located at 433 South Dearborn St. To make an appointment, call the number in the photo.

She Sees Sea Serpents
The Buckingham Fountain

What do you call seahorses that aren't exactly seahorses because they have the front end of a horse and the back end of a sea monster? According to city planner and urban designer Edward H. Bennett, you can call them Wisconsin, Illinois, Indiana, and Michigan.

When is a seahorse not quite a seahorse?

Let me explain.

Bennett designed the Clarence Buckingham Memorial Fountain to represent Lake Michigan, with four sea monsters symbolizing the four states that touch the lake. The design was also influenced by the Latona Basin in Louis XIV's gardens at Versailles. Sculptor Marcel Loyau built the sea monsters out of bronze. The rest of the fountain is Georgia pink marble.

Opened in 1927, the fountain was commissioned by Kate Buckingham, who dedicated the structure to the people of Chicago in memory of her brother, Clarence. She also set up an endowment to cover repair and upkeep.

Buckingham Fountain is one of the largest in the world, measuring 280 feet in diameter and featuring 134 jets powered by three pumps. Its water display is spectacular, but to me, those seahorses-that-aren't-quite-seahorses are the true curiosity. The sea monsters (and the rest of the fountain, of course) are located at Columbus Drive and Congress Parkway in Grant Park.

We Want . . . a Shrubbery!!

Hedgerow Sculpture

If you visit Grant Park, be on the lookout for a most peculiar hedge. It's not green. It's not trimmed into a neat rounded shape. In fact, it would be rejected by Monty Python's Knights Who Say Ni. Why? Because it's not a shrubbery at all. It's an assortment of automobile parts—mufflers, metal bumpers, springs, tailpipes, headlights, tail-lights, and rotors—assembled into a rectangular work of art.

Created by installation artist Lucy Slivinski, *Hedgerow* was designed for Artists and Automobiles, an art project presented by Allstate and the Chicago Department of Cultural Affairs in 2006. Chicago artists traveled to Allstate's research and training facility in Wheeling, Illinois, where they selected parts from totaled cars. The parts were delivered to their studios, where they set to work making treasure out of junk.

In addition to Slivinski's eye-catching hedge, the project included a glass bench made from car windows and the sides of a minivan, a huge red lily and nymph structure made from the parts of five separate automobiles, and a 9-foot-tall moose sculpture made of car bumpers (see "But Where's Rocky the Flying Squirrel?" in the Near North chapter of this book).

Hedgerow is on the southwest corner of Columbus Drive and Congress Avenue in Grant Park. Some of the other Artists and Automobile sculptures are located nearby.

One man's junk is another man's . . . um . . . hedge?

Lawyer, Playwright, Cherub!
The Boy on a Dolphin Statue

In the lobby of the Chicago Hilton there's a bronze statue of a little boy riding a dolphin. He and his dolphin used to reside at the lavish Stevens Hotel on Michigan Avenue, which opened in 1927 and went bankrupt during the Great Depression.

The statue was at the Stevens because the boy's father owned the hotel. The boy and his two brothers posed for statues that were

Whoop-ee-ti-yi-o! Get along, little dolphin!

placed in fountains on either side of the lobby. The other statue portrayed a boy holding a large fish while another boy stood next to him, pointing at the fish.

According to the grandson of Frederick C. Hibbard, the sculptor who created the statues, William Stevens modeled for the statue of the boy holding the fish. John was the boy standing next to him. Richard James posed for the statue of the cherub on the dolphin.

All three boys went on to become successful lawyers. Richard James—the boy on the dolphin—was also a playwright. Of the three, however, John made the biggest name for himself. Perhaps you've heard of U.S. Supreme Court justice John Paul Stevens?

The Chicago Hilton is located at 720 South Michigan Ave.

Leapin' Lizards!
Sue the Dinosaur

Like the promotional brochure says, the lady has a "killer smile." She could be described as statuesque (13 feet high at the hips) and well-preserved (most of her 200-plus bones are in excellent condition). Did I mention that she has been dead for sixty-seven million years?

I say "she," but scientists don't actually know whether the *Tyrannosaurus rex* whose skeleton is on display at the Field Museum was male or female. Sue was named for fossil hunter Sue Hendrickson, who discovered the dinosaur's remains at a dig site in South Dakota in 1990.

Sue has the distinction of being the largest, most complete, and best preserved T. rex fossil found to date. Field Museum technicians spent more than 25,000 hours preparing her bones for display (roughly the equivalent of one person working fifteen years, full-time).

The 5-foot-long skull mounted on the body in the display is a cast replica of the real skull, which is too heavy (at 600 pounds) to place on the steel frame holding the rest of the body together. The actual skull—complete with fifty-eight teeth ranging in length from 7½ to 12 inches—is displayed in a separate exhibit.

★ ★

Sue the Dinosaur is the largest, most complete, and best preserved T. rex fossil found to date.

It's no wonder that people flock to the museum to see Sue and have their picture taken with her. Who could resist that dazzling smile?

The Field Museum is located at 1400 South Lake Shore Dr. (Lake Shore Drive and East Roosevelt Road). For more information, call (312) 922-9410 or visit www.fieldmuseum.org.

At Home on the "Caribbean Reef"

Nickel the Sea Turtle

The faces of turtles remind me of E.T., the extraterrestrial from Steven Spielberg's movie. The faces of larger turtles are easiest to see, and sometimes they wear an eerily human expression. Case in point: Nickel the green sea turtle at Shedd Aquarium. Now that I think of it, she doesn't so much resemble E.T. as this kid I knew in third grade. But that's neither here nor there.

Unlike E.T., Nickel came from Florida. When Nickel arrived at Shedd Aquarium in 2003, veterinarians discovered a coin lodged in her esophagus. A nickel was removed from her throat, and thenceforth she was known as Nickel.

The turtle also had a deep gash from a boat propeller in her carapace (upper shell). She couldn't submerge or paddle her hind feet. The injury permanently affected her buoyancy, and she can't be released back into the wild.

Fortunately, the wounded sea turtle has a home in the Caribbean Reef exhibit. Green sea turtles (*Chelonia mydas*) are endangered, and Nickel's presence allows the aquarium to share an important message about conservation.

Shedd Aquarium is located at 1200 South Lake Shore Dr. For more information, call (312) 939-2438 or visit www.sheddaquarium.org.

This turtle's name was decided by the toss of a coin.
JODI J. BROWN

Now That's Italian!

Balbo Monument

Do you know who Balbo was? I took a poll, and 80 percent of the respondents thought he was the diminutive hero of *The Hobbit* (for the record, that's Bilbo, not Balbo).

So let's get this straight.

In May 1933 Chicago opened the Century of Progress World's Fair. One of the fair's highlights took place when Italian aviator Italo Balbo and a squadron of "flying boats" concluded a historic flight from Rome to Chicago by landing with great fanfare on Lake Michigan near the fairgrounds. In honor of Balbo's journey, Chicago renamed a street "Balbo Drive."

Huzzah!

But wait, there's more. Enter Benito Mussolini, Il Duce himself. Balbo helped bring Mussolini to power in Italy, so Il Duce wanted to do something special for him. Following Balbo's historic flight, Mussolini plucked an 18-foot Roman column dating from the second century AD and shipped it to Chicago, where it was erected in front of the Italian pavilion at the World's Fair. The inscription, carved in Italian, read in part, "Fascist Italy, with the sponsorship of Benito Mussolini, presents to Chicago a symbol and memorial in honor of the Atlantic Squadron led by Balbo."

It was a really big deal at the time, something the city could be proud of. Then Mussolini became Adolf Hitler's new best friend.

In spite of the monumental falling out between Italy and America during World War II, the Balbo monument remained in place. It has been suggested more than once over the years that something should be done about Chicago's "tributes to Fascism" (the street and the monument). Those who disagree point out that Balbo actually expressed disapproval of Italy's alliance with Germany. (His plane was shot down by friendly fire in 1940, possibly under direct orders from Mussolini.)

* *

And so, for now, the Balbo Monument remains on its original site, where it continues to deteriorate. The Italian pavilion is long gone and, like the cheese in that "Farmer in the Dell" song, the monument stands alone. You can find it at 1400 South Museum Campus Dr., just north of McCormick Place.

Ode to an Address
2120 South Michigan Avenue

How many famous street addresses can you list? Let's start with 1600 Pennsylvania Avenue, home of the president of the United States. Then there's 10 Downing Street, home of the prime minister of Great Britain. And don't forget 221b Baker Street, home of fictional detective Sherlock Holmes.

But what about 2120 South Michigan Avenue? Whose address is that, you ask? Some might say it's the address of the blues. Today the building is home to Willie Dixon's Blues Heaven Foundation, but the address became famous back in the 1950s and 1960s, when Chess Records was in the house.

The names of people who recorded at 2120 South Michigan Avenue reads like a who's who of rhythm and blues: Chuck Berry, Bo Diddley, Muddy Waters, Little Walter Jacobs, John Lee Hooker, Etta James, Howlin' Wolf, Buddy Guy. Oh, and there was this band called the Rolling Stones.

During sessions at the South Michigan Avenue address in 1964, the Stones recorded such blockbuster hits as "It's All Over Now," "Time Is on My Side," and "(I Can't Get No) Satisfaction." While they were there, they laid down tracks for an instrumental number—"2120 South Michigan Avenue"—immortalizing the address.

Willie Dixon once led the house band at Chess, played bass, and produced and sometimes wrote for the label. A key figure in the creation of Chicago blues, Dixon was instrumental (pun intended) in linking the blues and rock and roll. His Blues Heaven Foundation is a nonprofit dedicated to preserving the music and memory of the blues.

★ ★

For more information or to arrange a tour of 2120 South Michigan Avenue, call (312) 808-1286 or visit http://bluesheaven.com/tours.

A poster outside 2120 South Michigan Avenue
pays tribute to the city's blues stars.

"El" on Wheels

The El

Faster than a speeding taxi! Powered by a steam locomotive! Able to loop around tall buildings on a single track! Look! Up in the sky! It's a clanking, thundering, screeching monster on wheels! It's the El!

Yes, it's the El (or "L") . . . that strange form of transportation with powers and abilities far beyond those of a horse-drawn street-car. Don't laugh. That was important back in 1892 when Chicago's first elevated line—the South Side Rapid Transit Railroad—went into operation. On its inaugural trip from Congress Street to 39th Street, passengers toasted each other with champagne and marveled that they could now travel the 3.6 miles in ten minutes instead of thirty.

The Lake Street "L" burst onto the tracks a year later, followed by the Metropolitan West Side "L," the first to use electric traction

The El: able to loop around tall buildings on a single track!

technology. By 1898 a complete set of elevated tracks circled Chicago's central business district. The Northwestern "L" opened for service a couple years after that.

Originally known as the Union Loop (it was owned by the Union Elevated Railroad), the area encircled by the "L" eventually became simply "The Loop." Today the name is synonymous with Chicago.

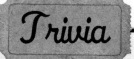

The world's first skyscraper, the Home Insurance Building, was built in Chicago in 1885. It was ten stories tall.

2

Near North

The Near North Side is bordered by the Chicago River on the south, Lake Michigan on the east, and North Avenue on the north.

Pioneer Court, a small plaza near the junction of the Chicago River and Upper Michigan Avenue, marks the spot where Jean Baptiste Pointe du Sable set up a trading post in 1780. Markers in the pavement along Michigan Avenue denote the approximate site of Fort Dearborn, erected in 1803.

The Near North Side also features Chicago's largest shopping district, the Magnificent Mile. The Mag Mile connects the business district with the Gold Coast, Chicago's wealthiest neighborhood. The Mag Mile is located in Streeterville, which includes some of Chicago's tallest skyscrapers as well as one of the city's most popular tourist spots, Navy Pier.

The River North neighborhood has been through a number of incarnations, starting out as an industrial area and later becoming a warehouse district. It now offers a mix of trendy cafes, art galleries, theme restaurants, and nightclubs.

Buildings on the North Side that are sure to catch your eye include the neo-Gothic Tribune Tower, the residential/commercial complex called Marina City, the castlelike Water Tower, and the enormously impressive Merchandise Mart.

If you want to know everything there is to know about the history of the Windy City, the Chicago History Museum awaits you on North Clark Street.

★ ★

"Tales from the Crypt"
The Couch Tomb

To quote the *Chicago Tribune:* "Of the stones and memorials which once marked the resting places of the countless thousands buried in what is now Lincoln Park, the tomb of the Couch family alone remains. The vault, surrounded by great trees, stands there in the park, a subject of curiosity to visitors." Although these words could

Who's buried in the Couch tomb—
and why is it in Lincoln Park?

easily have appeared in a current issue of the newspaper, they actually were published on February 11, 1892.

The Couch family built the limestone mausoleum in 1857 or 1858, when the property was part of City Cemetery. By the early 1870s, most of the cemetery's remains had been relocated so that the land could be used as a park. The Couch tomb stayed where it was, perhaps because it was too expensive to move or perhaps because the influential Couch family objected to moving it.

Another "subject of curiosity" concerning this monument is the fact that no one can say for certain how many people are buried inside, or who they are. (The stone tablets that flank the door to the vault are blank, and there is no lettering anywhere except COUCH over the entrance.) Folks are pretty sure that wealthy hotelier Ira Couch is in there, but beyond that, accounts vary. Ira may be alone, or he may be interred with anywhere from seven to thirteen other people. When his brother James died in 1892, an effort was made to open the tomb but the door was rusted shut. James was buried elsewhere.

The Couch monument is located in Lincoln Park, which stretches along the lakefront from Ardmore Avenue (in Edgewater) south to North Avenue. For more information, visit http://hiddentruths.north western.edu/couch/tomb.html.

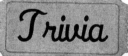

Trivia

The first Ferris wheel made its debut in Chicago at the 1893 World's Columbian Exposition. Today, Navy Pier is home to a fifteen-story Ferris wheel, modeled after the original one.

★ ★

Hedge Trimmers, Beware!
The Great Chain

When Revolutionary War historians mention the "Great Chain," they're referring to a chain forged at Sterling Ironworks in New York. The Great Chain—also called the West Point Chain, General Washington's Watch Chain, and the Putnam Chain (for Colonel Rufus

Can this chain keep enemy ships from reaching
the Chicago History Museum?

Putnam)—was approximately 500 yards long. Its links were 2 feet long and 2¼ inches thick, and each link weighed 114 pounds.

In 1778 American forces stretched the Great Chain across the Hudson River in an effort to stop the British from reaching inland forts. Today links from the original chain are on display at Trophy Point in New York.

Let me explain why I'm including this information in a book called *Chicago Curiosities*. It has to do with the Chicago History Museum—specifically, with the plaza on the east side of the museum. If you search in the ornamental yew border next to the plaza, you'll find a chain.

It seems that in the 1880s, junk dealer John C. Abbey began selling iron links that he claimed had come from the Great Chain. Buyers included Chicago sweets manufacturer Charles Frederick Gunther,

Separated at Birth?

In a city as big as Chicago, it's not unusual to have two babies with the same last name born on the same day. But what about two babies with the same first, middle, and last name? It happened on February 25, 1985, at Northwestern Memorial Hospital. Two couples, who were not related and had never met, both had the last name Heyman. They chose first and middle names for their baby sons for very different reasons—yet both couples chose the first name David and the middle name Charles. When asked to comment, the parents described the whole thing as "bizarre" and "pretty wild." No word on whether the two boys ever encountered each other again.

who was putting together a museum on Wabash Avenue. For several decades, the Chicago History Museum proudly displayed these links as a section of the original Great Chain. In the 1960s, the links were proven to be a fraud. They were relocated to the sidewalk outside the Chicago Historical Society's permanently sealed rear door.

The giant chain links now reside in a heap, unlabeled, outside the museum. In the same set of hedges, you'll find a big blob of melted metal, the remains of a hardware store destroyed in the 1871 fire.

The Chicago History Museum is located at 1601 North Clark St. For more information, call (312) 642-4600 or visit http://chicago history.org.

Instruments of Torture or Medical Breakthroughs?
You Make the Call
International Museum of Surgical Science

Does the thought of trepanation fill you with trepidation? It should, unless you're perfectly comfortable with the idea of having a hole drilled into your skull. Trepanation may be the oldest surgical procedure for which there's clear, physical evidence. That's why the International Museum of Surgical Science displays instruments used in this ancient therapy, along with a few skulls on which the technique was practiced.

While wandering through the elegant lakeside mansion that houses the museum, you might find yourself examining the splendid interior architecture even as you investigate the triumphs and traumas of medical history. My personal favorites among the relics are the Austrian amputation saw with reversible blade (ca. 1500); replicas of surgical knives from around 1300 to 1400; and the polio exhibit, featuring an iron lung used before the 1950s. (I'm old enough to remember when the polio vaccine was first administered in my hometown.) Then there are the numerous murals that graphically depict operating room scenes from hell . . . I mean, from days gone by.

There's more—including an eighteenth-century apothecary,

Try popping a wheelie in this bad boy—
a wheelchair from around 1780.

orthopedics wing, ophthalmology section, radiology room, and dentistry exhibit (not for the faint of heart or sensitive of tooth). To top it all off, they have a replica of Napoleon Bonaparte's death mask. (Bonaparte supported scientific research and its application to medicine.)

The International Museum of Surgical Science is located at 1524 North Lake Shore Dr. For more information call (312) 642-6502 or visit www.imss.org.

★ ★

Plant It and They Will Come
City Farm

Ah, life in the Big City: towers scraping the sky, horns blaring, traffic jamming, people hustling and bustling, thirty varieties of tomatoes growing . . . Wait a minute. Thirty varieties of tomatoes? This is Chicago. Mr. Green Jeans doesn't live here. So what are thirty varieties of tomatoes and a hundred types of organic vegetables and herbs doing in a 1.25-acre vacant lot about a mile and a half from Chicago's tallest skyscrapers?

Ask recycling pioneer Ken Dunn, who in 2000 established City Farm at Division and Clybourn. It's Dunn's belief that the city's tens

City Farm: A hundred types of organic vegetables and herbs can't be wrong!

of thousands of empty lots should be cleared, cultivated, and turned into urban farms. City Farm is an example of how unused property in economically challenged neighborhoods can be converted into fresh produce, jobs, and learning opportunities. In recent years the City Farm program has expanded to include other lots.

Their motto could be "Plant it and they will come."

Food grown at City Farm is served at numerous Chicago restaurants, where chefs rave about its flavor and beauty, and sold to the public from an on-site market stand. The farm also hosts group visits and events. Thousands have come through City Farm's different gardens to be trained or to learn about food.

Spring, summer, and early fall are the best times of the year to stop by and enjoy the sights, smells, and tastes of City Farm. In the winter it looks a bit forlorn, like most things. Be sure to say hello to Mr. Green Jeans!

City Farm is located at 1204 North Clybourn Ave. For more information, call (773) 821-1351, e-mail cityfarm@resourcecenterchicago .org, or visit www.resourcecenterchicago.org/70thfarm.html.

Now We're Cookin'
Culinary Curiosity Exhibition

I first realized I was "old" when I had to admit to my children that people didn't have microwave ovens when I was a kid. I wish the Culinary Curiosity exhibition at Kendall College had existed back then. After looking at the vegetable or leaf tobacco cutter (ca. 1890) or the six-hole Staple Favorite steel range (ca. 1895–1915), I would have come away thinking "Hey, I'm not that old after all!"

You might wonder what possessed Kendall College to create an exhibit featuring food-related tools from nineteenth- and early twentieth-century America, eighteenth-century Europe, and a number of other cultures. But it's not about what possessed the college; it's about a collection possessed by Mel and Janet Mickevic. Mr. Mickevic, a retired food scientist, inherited antique food-preparation equipment

★ ★

In the 1800s you had to stick your hand in the oven to test the temperature.

from his parents and from his wife's father, Justin Alikonis, a candy technologist who directed research for the Beich Company.

The Mickevics' goal in donating their collection of 300 objects to the exhibit was to inspire people to develop new products to solve today's problems, just as the inventors of the equipment in the collection solved the problems of their day. Included are agricultural implements, commercial equipment, and items used by the home cook.

One of my favorites is the counterweight spit jack engine from around 1800 England. This device, with its gears and weights, replaced caged animals (mostly short-legged, long-bodied dogs bred to run on a wheel) or servant-boys (called "jacks") who turned meat-roasting spits in front of the fire. I also like the fireless cooker from 1905. It resembles a wooden blanket chest but functions a bit like a modern-day Crock-Pot (no, they didn't have Crock-Pots when I was a child either).

Ah, the good old days, when you had to put your hand in the oven for as long as tolerable in order to determine if the temperature was right . . .

Kendall College is located at 900 North Branch St. For more information about the Culinary Curiosity exhibition, call (866) 667-3344 or visit www.culinarycuriosity.org.

Get on Your Soapbox!
Bughouse Square

If you've ever been told to "get off your soapbox," you'll be glad to know that there's an annual event where people are encouraged to get *on* a soapbox to present their views.

It all started in the early part of the twentieth century, when Washington Square Park became a center for free speech in Chicago. Speakers and hecklers often got really wound up, and people began to refer to the park as Bughouse Square ("bughouse" being slang for a mental health facility).

Bughouse Square reached its heyday in the 1920s and 1930s. On any given night as many as 2,000 people might gather in the park. The core group of orators consisted of individuals on the political left. Many were affiliated with the Industrial Workers of the World (IWW), a radical labor organization.

In the 1940s and 1950s, Bughouse Square was more of a tourist attraction than anything else, and by the early 1960s, not much was going on in the park. That changed in the mid-1980s, when a group of Chicago leftists joined forces with staff from the nearby Newberry Library.

A new kind of Bughouse Square Debates was established in 1986. Typically held in July, it's a freewheeling event that involves three soapboxes and a lot of shouting. The audience can move around, engage the speaker, or call out comments and questions. Orators have to think on their feet, listen, and respond. Soapbox speeches in the recent past addressed such controversial issues as gun control, immigrant rights, the donation of tax dollars to houses of worship, and the parking situation in Chicago.

Bughouse Square is located at 901 North Clark St. For more information about the Bughouse Square Debates, call (312) 255-3700.

During the Bughouse Square Debates, speakers present their arguments on a soapbox-size stage.
BOB MATTER

When More Is More

More Cupcakes

Remember the days when cupcakes were considered poor substitutes for "real" cakes? Back then, you could count the number of different cupcake flavors on one hand. Ditto for the frosting.

If you're ready to come into the twenty-first century, pay a visit to More Cupcakes. Start slowly, if you like, perhaps with a dark chocolate cupcake with cream filling, topped with chocolate ganache. That's just the tip of the iceberg, of course.

Allow your taste buds to fantasize about salted caramel, red velvet, gingerbread lemon, strawberry rhubarb, or s'more cupcakes. Now it's time to move on to the line of savory cupcakes. Imagine, if you can, bacon maple, peach bacon BBQ, blue cheese walnut praline, or feta persimmon.

Going way out on a limb, I ask you to consider the Bloody Mary, which consists of tomato cake and vodka buttercream, garnished with chopped celery. Not exotic enough? How about a cupcake with bacon frosting, topped with shaved fresh white truffles? There's even a foie gras cupcake.

More Cupcakes is located at 1 East Delaware Place. For "More" information, call (312) 951-0001 or visit www.morecupcakes.com.

Small World

Cool Globes

It really is a small world after all—5 feet in diameter to be precise. I stumbled upon it right there on the sidewalk near More Cupcakes at 1 East Delaware Place.

The world, in this case, is a deep, dark, metallic blue color and covered with tiny yellow dots. The continents are raised up slightly from the surface. There are small, black, circular objects placed in pairs at various places on the world. On top are what appear to be small solar panels.

Joe Compean's *One Earth* from the
2007 Cool Globes exhibit.

A plaque on the base is titled AWARENESS and is followed by a quote from astronaut James Lovell about how the earth looks from outer space—uninhabited, with no boundaries marked on it. The remaining text explains that as the crew of Spaceship Earth, we all need to help steer the planet in the right direction. Finally, at the bottom of the plaque, we see the words ARTIST: JOE COMPEAN, "ONE EARTH" followed by a list of sponsors.

I decided to find out more about this "small world." As it turns out, it was one of 125 globes in a public art exhibit, "Cool Globes: Hot Ideas for a Cooler Planet," sponsored by a nonprofit corporation. Artists from around the world were asked to decorate the globes with solutions to global warming. Placed on display in the summer of 2007, the globes were designed to inspire individuals and organizations to take action.

Compean's contribution to the exhibition is truly a curiosity worthy of exploration. As he describes it, *One Earth* "is a celestial sphere with the constellations represented on the surface of the globe as they would appear from space. Each star is illuminated with a fiber optic rod that lights up at night. The globe also has six stereoscopic viewers (for people to look through) installed along what is perceived as the celestial equator. Each viewer has one of my stereoscopic-slide photographs, depicting various locations on the earth. The stars and viewers are lit from inside the globe by solar powered lights."

Ah ha! Now I know what those odd black objects are: stereoscopic viewers! Cool globe indeed!

For more information about the Cool Globes project, visit www.coolglobes.com. For more about the work of Chicago photographer and artist Joe Compean, visit www.bludomain5.com/compean.

Trivia

The Lincoln Park Zoo, one of only three free major zoos in the United States, is the country's oldest public zoo, with an annual attendance of three million people.

What Is That Castellated Monstrosity?

Historic Water Tower

So you're driving along North Michigan Avenue, staring up at all the
impossibly tall modern buildings, when suddenly you see . . . a castle.
A castle? Is it the home of some eccentric English noble who settled
in Chicago once upon a time? Nope, it's the Historic Water Tower.

The Historic Water Tower survived the Great
Fire, but can it survive thousands of tourists?

Designed by architect William W. Boyington, the water tower was built in 1869 out of Joliet limestone blocks. It originally housed a 138-foot standpipe, 3 feet in diameter. Two years after the water tower was erected, the Great Fire of 1871 blew through town, leveling all public buildings in the area except for the tower and the Chicago Avenue pumping station. Standing tall and proud above the ruins, the water tower became a symbol of the "I Will" spirit of the Chicago people.

The tower was designed to resemble a medieval castle, and that it does. Oscar Wilde reportedly described it as "a castellated monstrosity with pepper boxes stuck all over it," but others view it as romantic and stately. At 154 feet tall, the building once towered (sorry) over surrounding structures. These days, it's dwarfed by nearby skyscrapers such as the John Hancock Center (1,127 feet).

The Historic Water Tower is located at 806 North Michigan Ave. Inside you'll find Chicago's official photograph gallery. The Chicago Water Works Pumping Station at 163 East Pearson at Michigan Avenue still pumps water for the city but also serves as a Visitor Welcome Center, housing a restaurant and live theater space. For more information, call (312) 742-0808 or visit http://egov.cityofchicago.org /tourism.

"Hi, Bob!"
Bob Newhart Sculpture

The Bob Newhart Show ran on CBS from 1972 to 1978. In the show, Bob Newhart (a native of Chicago suburb Oak Park) played successful psychologist Bob Hartley, who lived in Chicago with his wife, Emily (Suzanne Pleshette). Each week, Bob interacted with his needy neighbor, a brash receptionist, various neurotic patients, and the other tenants in his office building—most of whom greeted him with "Hi, Bob!"

Now you, too, can say "Hi, Bob!" Not to Bob Newhart himself, but to a bronze replica of him seated in an armchair next to a bronze couch. Installed in 2004, the statue was originally placed near Bob Hartley's fictional office building at 430 North Michigan Ave. Like both Newhart and Hartley, the statue has since "moved on." It now resides in a park in front of Navy Pier.

I've never been a patient of the "real" Bob Hartley, so I can't speak to his skills as a psychologist. From personal experience, however, I can tell you that the bronze version of Hartley is a great listener. As for the bronze couch, well, let's just say it made me very uncomfortable.

If you go to Navy Pier, be sure to stop and say "Hi, Bob!"

The Dill Pickle Club

According to owner John A. "Jack" Jones, the Dill Pickle Club (or Dil Pickle Club) was formed as a "center where any idea or work would be given a respectful hearing." To that end, in 1915, Jones purchased a ramshackle building at 10 Tooker Place, just off Dearborn Street. To get there, people were told to go "through the hole in the wall down Tooker Alley, to the green lite over the orange door."

Dill Picklers included academics, anarchists, con men, hoboes, prostitutes, religious zealots, social workers, and socialists as well as renowned Chicago writers such as Carl Sandburg and Upton Sinclair. The Pickler spirit was captured in the motto on the door: "Step High, Stoop Low, Leave Your Dignity Outside." Although the original location vanished many years ago, attempts are occasionally still made to revive the club.

What, Nothing from the Rock of Gibraltar?

Tribune Tower

You have to get up close and personal with the Tribune Tower if you want to see what I think is the most curious (and coolest) thing about it. Incorporated into the outside walls at street level are rock fragments and stones from famous locations all over the world, including the Greek Parthenon, the Egyptian pyramids, the Alamo, the Great Wall of China, John Brown's Fort, the Berlin Wall, and a Viking monument from the Malar Lake Valley of Sweden.

Reading the labels takes you on a trip through time and across oceans, to places you've been and places you've only dreamed of

★ ★

seeing. On one section of the wall, for example, I saw stones from
Beaumaris Castle in Wales (AD 1295), Tainitzkaya Tower, Fort Sumter,
Union Stock Yards Gate, and Bunker Hill.

Modeled after the Button Tower of the Rouen Cathedral in France,
the Trib Tower was completed in 1925. It is located at 435 North
Michigan Ave.

Stones from famous locations are embedded in the
walls of the Tribune Tower at street level.

A Crime Writer's Surprise Ending

Eugene (Guy) Izzi, age forty-three, was an award-winning crime novelist with a new book coming out. The last thing anyone expected on December 14, 1996, was for him to be discovered dangling by his neck from the open window of his fourteenth-story North Michigan Avenue office.

Had someone murdered the man who wrote so eloquently about Chicago's "dark side"? It seemed unlikely that anyone could have tied a rope around the neck of the 6-foot-tall, 200-pound Izzi and pushed him out the window. There were rumors of a publicity stunt gone wrong, but clues that included an antidepressant found in Izzi's system led to a ruling of suicide.

But Where's Rocky the Flying Squirrel?
Moose Sculpture

At first glance, I thought the chrome creature in Pioneer Court was a cow. As we know, Chicago is all about cows. But a number of things about the welded-steel wonder were decidedly unbovine. I realized that it looked a whole lot more like Bullwinkle than Bessie.

Created from automobile bumpers by sculptor John Kearney, this work of art is nearly 9 feet tall and equally long. Kearney, who honed his welding skills as a sailor in World War II, contributed *Moose* to Chicago's Artists and Automobiles public art display in the summer of 2006. Kearney's other "steel bumper work" includes horses, giraffes, zebras, and the statue of the Tin Man in Oz Park. A smaller moose was on exhibit at the Chicago Cultural Center for a time.

★ ★

When I happened upon *Moose,* he was corralled by a single-chain next to a construction project on Michigan Avenue. I wondered if someone had confined him for fear that he might bolt at the noise made by the equipment. He seemed calm, however. And shiny. Very shiny.

Pioneer Court is located near the junction of the Chicago River and Upper Michigan Avenue in Chicago's Magnificent Mile.

What if the Tin Man had a pet moose?

"Double Cheeseborger Is Better!"
Billy Goat Tavern

As the old-timers tell it, back in the 1930s a goat fell off a passing truck and wandered into a tavern owned by William Sianis. Sianis "adopted" the goat, then grew a goatee, adopted a nickname—"Billy Goat"—and renamed the bar the Billy Goat Tavern.

Of course, that's not all Sianis did, as Chicago Cubs fans know. In 1945 he brought his goat to the World Series at Wrigley Field.

The Billy Goat Tavern played a central role in a popular *Saturday Night Live* skit.

★ ★

Trivia

The game of 16-inch softball, played without gloves, was invented in Chicago. The larger ball didn't travel as far, so it was ideal for neighborhood ball fields and school playgrounds.

Following complaints about the goat's odor, Sianis and his companion were ejected. The Cubs lost the Series, and Sianis sent a note to Cubs owner P. K. Wrigley saying, "Who stinks now?" The rumor began to spread that Sianis had cursed the team, and the Cubs have not appeared in a World Series since.

The Billy Goat Tavern is also famous as the setting for one of *Saturday Night Live*'s most beloved sketches. When I had lunch there not too long ago, I saw owner Sam Sianis, nephew of William, flipping burgers on the grill. I ordered a cheeseburger. "Double cheeseborger is better!" exclaimed the guy behind the counter. I don't know if it was "better" than a single would have been, but it was pretty darn good.

The Billy Goat Tavern is located at 430 North Michigan Ave., downstairs from the main Michigan Avenue walking area. Take the stairs at the northwest corner of Hubbard and Michigan. The restaurant also has several other locations. For more information, visit www.billygoattavern.com.

High Steaks?

Weber Grill Restaurant

The best thing about the giant Weber grill affixed to the building on North State Street is that it is bright red. From one angle, it looks kind of like a mammoth tomato with legs. Inside the restaurant, Weber grills dominate not only the kitchen but the dining room decor. Outside on the patio, the planters are made out of Weber grills.

Where else can you put a grill if your apartment doesn't have a deck?

If there are any reality TV producers reading this, I have an idea for a new show: Contestants compete to see who can produce the best steak dinner using a huge grill attached to the second story of a building in downtown Chicago. Points are given not only for the quality of the food prepared, but for the level of creativity used in gaining access to the grill. Points are taken off for broken bones. We'll call the show *Playing for High Steaks.*

What? Not risky enough? Not offensive enough? Oh well.

The Weber Grill Restaurant is located at 539 North State St., between Grand Avenue and Ohio Street. For more information, call (312) 467-9696 or visit www.webergrillrestaurant.com/.

It's A-*maize*-ing!

Marina City

When architect Bertrand Goldberg designed the towers that now stand at 300 North State St., he wasn't thinking about the Prairie State's leading agricultural products. Goldberg wanted to build "a city within a city," a multifunctional complex with apartments, restaurants, banks, and parking spaces. He also wanted to depart from the monotony of rectangular steel skyscrapers and do something a bit different. After all, it was the 1960s, and going against the norm was . . . well . . . the norm.

So Goldberg's two buildings on the Chicago River were made of concrete with a cylindrical shape for less wind pressure. At sixty-one stories, they were two of the tallest and biggest concrete structures in the world at the time.

There was a marina beneath the complex, so it was officially called Marina City. Goldberg had intended the towers to resemble trees, but people quickly picked up on the fact that the tall, cylindrical buildings looked like giant corncobs (called "maize" by Native Americans). A nickname was born.

Fortunately, the presence of two giant corncobs isn't necessarily a

The towers of Marina City have a nickname. Can you guess what it is?

★ ★

bad thing in a city located in the heart of the Corn Belt. No word on any plans to drizzle gallons of melted butter down the sides of the towers.

For more information, visit www.marina-city.com or www.marina cityonline.com.

Super PEZ!
Merchant's Hall of Fame

Back in the 1950s, Joseph P. Kennedy decided to immortalize outstanding American merchants. And what better place to do this than in front of the Merchandise Mart, a property he owned in Chicago?

The Merchandise Mart encompasses 4.2 million square feet, spans two city blocks, and stands twenty-five stories tall. It's so big, it has its own zip code.

Outside the Mart, the Merchant's Hall of Fame honors eight men whose names or companies are known all across America: Marshall Field, Edward Albert Filene, George Huntington Hartford, Julius Rosenwald, John Wanamaker, Aaron Montgomery Ward, Robert Elkington Wood, and Frank Winfield Woolworth. Supersize bronze busts of these giants of merchandising are mounted on tall pillars.

Late-night TV host David Letterman likened these monuments to

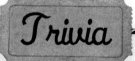

Trivia

The world's first giant mail-order enterprise was Montgomery Ward & Company, which started in Chicago just after the Great Fire of 1871. Montgomery Ward and Sears, also located in Chicago, dominated the mail-order business during its heyday between the 1890s and 1910s.

Giants of merchandising or monster PEZ dispensers?

PEZ dispensers, referring to the display as the "PEZ Hall of Fame." That may seem like an insult, but PEZ dispensers are part of popular culture in the United States and many other nations. Some people even collect them. Clearly the company that markets PEZ Candy (which dates back to the 1920s) is a superb merchandiser. I can imagine the merchant-busts nodding their approval.

The Merchant's Hall of Fame is located at 222 West Merchandise Mart Plaza.

The Value of Aesthetic Effectiveness
The Wind Blew Inn

Early in 1922 New Yorker Lillian Collier opened an art center called the Wind Blew Inn at 116 East Ohio St. in Chicago. The bob-haired and stockingless Miss Collier was on a mission: to bring Bohemianism—and "the value of aesthetic effectiveness"—to the city. She summed up her concerns about Chicago by observing that there were "too many folks just in from the corn belt. Really, they drive cows to pasture by here every morning."

Not everyone appreciated Collier's efforts. They complained that the interior of her place was barely lit by candles and there were nude statues. Neighbors grumbled about loud piano music at all hours of the night. The police raided the Wind Blew Inn twice in February, booking Collier as "keeper of a disorderly house."

"Just wait until I tell Mayor Thompson on you fellows!" she shouted the second time. "He will let me open up again." Apparently she was right. In March the *Chicago Tribune* reported that Collier herself had filed a complaint against the disorderly conduct of three of her guests.

In April 1922 a fire destroyed the Wind Blew Inn. The contents were valued at just $100, despite the "rare art" displayed on the premises.

3

North Side
(including Far North)

The North Side *extends north of downtown along the lakefront. This diverse, densely populated area offers almost any type of experience you would like to have.*

Lincoln Park, one of Chicago's wealthiest neighborhoods, contains a zoo, conservatory, outdoor theater, and rowing canal, along with the Peggy Notebaert Nature Museum and Oz Park. Lake View has the distinction of being the first gay village officially recognized as such by a civic body. Wrigley Field, home of the Chicago Cubs, is also located here.

North Center, settled mostly by Germans in the latter part of the nineteenth century and early twentieth century, today contains a mix of retailers, restaurants, theater, music, and service-oriented businesses. The influence of European immigrants is still felt in Avondale, with its sausage shops and Italian restaurants.

The Far North section contains Uptown, a popular entertainment destination and the location of Graceland Cemetery, final resting place of such notables as Augustus Dickens (younger brother of Charles), John Kinzie (first permanent white settler of Chicago), and Marshall Field (giant of commerce).

Lincoln Square is known for excellent restaurants and shopping. West Ridge is home to the Midwest's largest Hasidic community. More than eighty languages are spoken in Rogers Park, one of the most diverse neighborhoods in the country. Edgewater contains several beaches, and Andersonville, a former Swedish enclave, now has a large LGBT population.

★ ★

Heaven's Waiting Room
Shedd Memorial Chapel

It's as quiet as a tomb in here. That was my first thought as I entered the Shedd Memorial Chapel. My second thought was: *Brilliant, seeing as this is a tomb.*

Behind a set of heavy bronze doors flanked by two pedestals is the burial chamber of John Graves Shedd and family. The atrium is

The designs in the Shedd Chapel were inspired by marine life, a fitting tribute to a man who established an aquarium.

all white marble, with marble benches topped with leather cushions. A skylight bordered by an intricate vine pattern graces the ceiling. Bronze chairs line the walls, their backs featuring a seahorse-and-sand-dollar design. I am told that at sundown, light coming through a Tiffany stained-glass window makes the tomb look like it's underwater. That seems appropriate, given that Shedd—a millionaire and philanthropist—created the aquarium in Chicago that bears his name.

The John G. Shedd Memorial Chapel has a beautiful, haunting quality. I felt like I was in heaven's waiting room. I am not being flippant. The cool, quiet atrium feels otherworldly, yet you can still touch very solid marble and bronze. I had a sense that I was somewhere between the physical and spiritual realms, and would not have been surprised to come face to face with a real, live angel.

The John G. Shedd Memorial Chapel and burial chamber is located in Rosehill Cemetery at 5800 North Ravenswood Ave. The cemetery features memorials to fourteen Chicago mayors, sixteen Civil War generals, Nobel Prize winner and vice president Charles Gates Dawes, and businessmen Richard Sears, Montgomery Ward, Oscar Mayer, Milton Florsheim, and Jonas Kuppenheimer. For more information, call (773) 561-5940.

Of Trees and Trains
Bangs Monument

Shattered-tree monuments with severed branches are not uncommon in cemeteries. They were popular in late Victorian times as symbols of an unfinished life or a life cut short.

It could be said that George S. Bangs died before his time: According to the inscription on his limestone monument, he was 51 years, 8 months, and 27 days old. But his monument, located in Rosehill Cemetery, is not just an ordinary tree monument. A quick look at its base reveals something truly unique: a carving of a railroad car entering a tunnel.

Bangs was head of the Chicago mail system from 1871 to 1876.

During that time he worked tirelessly to organize a system of checks that would eliminate bottlenecks and locate the responsibility for delays in transmission of mail. He was instrumental in developing the Fast Mail service, which used special trains that traveled between major cities overnight, thus improving mail service from several weeks to several days.

Highly regarded by such notables as Abraham Lincoln and Ulysses S. Grant, Bangs was given a hero's funeral when he passed away in 1877. More than 600 postal clerks marched in a procession. All mail trains entering Chicago were draped in black in mourning.

Not many people have a carving of a train
at the base of their grave marker.

The railroad car monument dedicated to Bangs was paid for by postal clerks and other officials. In addition to informing visitors of his exact age when he died, the monument is also inscribed HIS CROWNING EFFORT, THE FAST MAIL.

Rosehill Cemetery and Mausoleum is located at 5800 North Ravenswood Ave. The George S. Bangs monument can be found in Section 6 near the northeast corner of the cemetery. Maps are available at the cemetery office. For more information, call (773) 561-5940.

Where Strawberry Shortcake Meets Rodan

Quake Collectibles

You're walking along North Lincoln Avenue, glancing at store windows as you pass by. Nothing really catches your eye until . . . wait! What was that? You back up. Is that . . .? Could it be . . .? It is! It's that toy stuffed-animal version of E.T. you had when you were a kid. And hold on! It's Frankenstein's monster and Pee Wee Herman and Smurfette and Darth Vader and C3PO and a Strawberry Shortcake lunchbox and this wooden turtle on wheels that makes a clucking sound when you pull it around the room. There's so much memorabilia, you can't take it all in—and that's just in the front window.

Congratulations, you've found Quake Collectibles!

A strong interest in pop culture and collectibles prompted shop

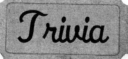

Trivia

Chicago has been the setting for some of television's most popular shows, including *Chicago Hope*, *ER*, *Perfect Strangers*, *The Bob Newhart Show*, *According to Jim*, *Family Matters*, and *Married with Children*.

Dr. Zaius from *Planet of the Apes* bakes cookies
while Dr. Kildare battles the Death Star!

owner David Gutterman to open Quake Collectibles about twenty
years ago. Gutterman himself began collecting vintage lunchboxes
and cereal boxes after college, and the store sort of took off from
there.

The sheer volume of merchandise stacked high on the shelves
is mind-boggling. Gutterman says that 90 percent of his inventory
"walks through the door." He's always buying. The other 10 percent

comes from estate sales, auctions, toy shows, flea markets, and thrift stores all over the country. It's impossible to wander through the store without smiling, laughing, and/or exclaiming, "Oh my gosh! I remember those!"

There they are, cheek by jowl: Barbie, G.I. Joe, Cookie Monster, Superman, Rodan, Elvis, Funshine Bear, She-Hulk, and Techno Spawn. It just doesn't get any better than that. Well, maybe it does. Just to the left of an Easy Bake Oven I spotted a twenty-six-piece Sesame Street tea set. I couldn't decide between that and a Dr. Kildare board game.

Quake Collectibles is located in Lincoln Square at 4628 North Lincoln Ave. For more information, call (773) 878-4288 or visit http://quakechicago.com.

Eel Power

It's a question many of us have been asking: How do you control a robot without using batteries or plugging it into the wall? Thankfully, physiologist Sandro Mussa-Ivaldi of Northwestern University's Rehabilitation Institute of Chicago came up with an answer back in 2001: He used an immature lamprey eel brain. It's so obvious, I can't believe I didn't think of it! The brain was removed from the eel, kept alive in a special solution, and attached with wires to a robot. Mussa-Ivaldi's ultimate goal is to create prostheses for people who are unable to control their limbs. More power to him!

A Trip Down Memory Lane(s)

Lincoln Square Bowling Alley

It was 1968. I was a high school senior. That year, I took bowling for physical education. Week in and week out, using a complex system that sharpened our math skills, my classmates and I catalogued our spares and strikes, our gutter balls and splits. Our score sheets chronicled the rise and fall of reputations and fortunes.

All this was on my mind decades later as I climbed the stairs to Lincoln Square Lanes, one of the very few second-story bowling alleys in Chicago. When I stepped through the doorway, I went back in time. There it all was: pine paneling, a prominent bar, fluorescent lighting, racks of cheap and/or ancient bowling balls, rickety old ball-return equipment, and—yes!—those old-timey score sheets.

Honest Abe is watching at Lincoln Square Lanes, so don't try anything funny with those score sheets!

Modern bowlers may prefer the automated scoring systems and funky graphics that brighten up most bowling establishments these days. In fact, computerized scoring is usually credited with reviving the general public's interest in the sport of bowling during the 1980s. However, there's nothing quite like taking pencil in hand and tallying the result—for better or worse—of each ball you throw.

I had to admire the mural stretching across the back wall, above the lanes. Centered in a setting of lush green trees and majestic purple mountains, Abraham Lincoln gazes down from a marble throne. Honest Abe wears a stern expression, as if chastening those who might be cheating at score-keeping.

Lincoln Square Lanes has been operating as a bowling alley since about 1918. The mural, discovered by the owner around 2003 while he was replacing ceiling tiles, may date from the 1930s. But this

Y Not Those of you who like to play games like "Where's Waldo?" might have fun looking for the Y in Chicago. I'm not talking about the YMCA or YWCA; I'm talking about the Y-shaped figure that appears on buildings and structures all over the city. This "Y in a circle" symbol—which can be colored and designed to suit individual tastes and needs, according to the code—represents the branches of the Chicago River as they come together at Wolf Point. The symbol is often integrated artistically into other designs. For examples, check out the steel framework of the Division Street bridge on the east side of Goose Island and the doorway of the Old Town School of Folk Music, at 4544 North Lincoln Ave.

★ ★

place—though decidedly retro—isn't completely mired in the past. Live music often provides a soundtrack for night bowling, and the annual New Year's Eve "Chuckle Bowl" typically features free pizza and entertainment such as an interactive game show, short films, and stand-up comedy.

Lincoln Square Lanes is located at 4874 North Lincoln Ave. For more information, call (773) 561-8191.

This Plaque Is Whack!
On This Site . . . Nothing Happened

Here a plaque, there a plaque, everywhere a bronze plaque. Chicago's ubiquitous bronze plaques mark sites where history was made or pay homage to people who shaped that history. Here are just a few examples:

- "Here stood Old Fort Dearborn 1803–1812." (360 North Michigan Ave.)
- "Near this site stood Kinzie Mansion 1784–1832." (401 North Michigan Ave.)
- "Near this site in 1833, the log store of John S. C. Hogan, was this section's only post office . . . " (northwest corner of Wacker Drive and Lake Street)
- "Near this site, the first United States Land Office was erected in 1835." (south side of Lake Street, east of Clark)

On the outside of a building on North Lincoln Avenue, between Eastwood and Wilson, is a bronze plaque that looks every bit as important as those described above. What significant historical event does it commemorate? Or does it honor a famous founding father? As it turns out, neither. The plaque reads:

ON THIS SITE

IN 1897 NOTHING

HAPPENED.

To see the plaque that commemorates a nonevent, go to 4613 North Lincoln Ave. in Lincoln Square, Ravenswood.

Thinking outside the Guidebook
Cornerstone Community Outreach

Typically, homeless shelters are not considered "tourist destinations." They aren't on the average person's list of leisure-time activities or places to visit when on vacation. Cornerstone Community Outreach (CCO) would like to change that.

According to the Chicago Coalition for the Homeless, 2.5 million to 3.5 million people throughout the United States experience homelessness in the course of a year. In Chicago, 74,149 people were homeless in the 2008–9 school year. Located in the Uptown neighborhood on Chicago's North Side, CCO has been providing services to the city's homeless population for more than twenty years. CCO's shelters and programs serve nearly 500 men, women, and children daily.

If you think that homelessness is far removed from you, and that you have nothing in common with people in homeless shelters, CCO encourages you to think again. And if you wonder what life is like at a homeless shelter, what sort of people live there, or what can be done about the problem, CCO invites you to come and see for yourself.

CCO is very open to visitors and to working with volunteers. They want to help people see this more "urban" side of Chicago. Guaranteed: It's an experience you won't forget.

If you want to stop by the shelter for a visit, call ahead to the coordinator's office at (773) 858-0836 to make arrangements. Consider getting involved in a project, even for a short time. Volunteers come from a wide variety of spiritual backgrounds and many different places, including Canada, Mexico, and Europe. For more information, visit www.ccolife.org/blog.

★ ★

Home Sweet Home
The Friendly Towers

Historically, towers aren't known for being friendly. Take the Tower of London, for example, or the Tower of Babel. Both were about as unfriendly as they could be. I've heard of ivory towers and clock towers, water towers and control towers—but friendly towers? Not so much.

Leave it to Chicago to provide welcoming, sociable towers.

A few residents of the Friendly Towers might remember when the ten-story building was called the Chelsea Hotel (1920s and 1930s) and later the Chelsea House (1960s). During the 1990s, Jesus People USA (JPUSA) bought it.

You remember the Jesus People, right? Those Christian hippies (or was it hippy Christians?) from the late 1960s and early 1970s, the ones some people called Jesus Freaks? Well, they've been living in Chicago since 1972. I'm not talking about a group of sixty-somethings wearing love beads, bell-bottom pants, and paisley shirts (although that might be entertaining). This is a group of about 500 people of all ages who live together at a single address on the North Side. (A core group of about thirty has been part of the community since the beginning.)

JPUSA is one of the world's largest single-site intentional communes in the United States. Using the book of Acts in the New Testament of the Bible as a guide, the Jesus People hold their goods and property in a common fund. The community functions as a resource to the church, a haven for people in need, and a learning experience.

JPUSA generates about 90 percent of its income from various community-owned-and-operated businesses. Around the Fourth of July, the community hosts the annual Cornerstone Festival—one of the largest Christian music and arts festivals in the country. Outreach is local, national, and global. Local outreach includes the Citizen Cafe and Skate Shop and the top three floors of the Friendly Towers, which are designated as affordable housing for senior citizens.

JPUSA, Citizen Cafe and Skate Shop, and the Friendly Towers are all located at 920 West Wilson Ave. For more information, call (773) 561-2450 or visit www.jpusa.org.

The Girl, the Ghost, the Gaffe

Inez Clarke Statue

It's hard to resist a good ghost story, and the one associated with the Inez Clarke monument at Graceland Cemetery is a doozy.

Consider the ingredients: A six-year-old girl is killed in 1880 during a storm while on a family picnic. Her parents commission a life-size statue for her grave. Placed in a glass box to protect it from the elements, the statue depicts a little girl sitting on a small stool. She wears a frilly dress and holds a parasol.

Over time, rumors abound that the grave is haunted. Disembodied weeping is heard. A ghostly child in nineteenth-century garments is seen playing near the monument. The statue vanishes during a violent thunderstorm, only to reappear in the glass case the next day.

It seems clear that Inez Clarke's troubled spirit is to blame. There's just one problem—well, maybe more than one. First of all, based on cemetery records, no one named Inez Clarke is buried in Graceland Cemetery. U.S. Census records contain no mention of such a child. Letters written by the people who were supposed to be the girl's parents indicate that they had only two daughters, both of whom were alive in 1910. The family has no idea who "Inez Clarke" might be.

So who's buried at the site? Cemetery records state that it's an eight-year-old boy named Amos Briggs. Inez, we hardly knew ye!

It has been suggested that the statue was originally placed in the cemetery as an advertisement for a monument maker. The longer it remained there, the larger and stronger the legend of Inez Clarke became. To this day, flowers and toys are frequently left at the base of the glass box.

Graceland Cemetery is located at 4001 North Clark St. To visit the *Inez Clarke* monument, enter Graceland Cemetery and take Main

Avenue to Graceland Avenue. Look for the Ayres monument, then walk eastward and begin looking for the glass-enclosed *Inez Clarke* monument (Section D). To contact the cemetery, call (773) 525-1105 or visit www.gracelandcemetery.org.

Inez Clarke: Mystery Girl
ANDY SPENCER

Munchkins in Chicago!

Parnell St. Aubin was sixteen years old when he played a Munchkin soldier in the 1939 movie classic *The Wizard of Oz*. At 43 inches tall, he was the tiniest of the Munchkin soldiers.

When production of Munchkinland scenes ended, St. Aubin moved back home to Chicago. In December 1947 he met Mary Ellen Burbach, a Little Person who was portraying one of Santa's elves at Goldblatt's department store.

Parnell and Mary Ellen were married. Together they created the Midget Club—first on South Kedzie Avenue and later on West 63rd Street. The club operated from 1948 to 1982.

Silence!

The Dexter Graves Grave

When you first see the robed, hooded figure, you almost expect it to slowly reach out a bony hand and point a finger at you—like the Ghost of Christmas Yet to Come pointing at Ebenezer Scrooge. But the figure doesn't move. It stands motionless before a polished black slab of granite, its face partly hidden by one arm.

In *A Christmas Carol,* the Ghost of Christmas Yet to Come didn't speak. Neither does this statue. That's a good thing, especially given that it's called *Eternal Silence.* What I really like about this mute, still figure is the fact that it marks the cemetery plot of a man whose last name was . . . get ready for it . . . Graves.

In 1831 Dexter Graves brought the first colony—a group of thirteen families from Ohio—to Chicago. He owned and ran a log cabin hotel called the Mansion House. When he died in 1844, his son commissioned sculptor Lorado Taft to do a monument. Taft is best remembered for his fountains, but anyone who has seen *Eternal Silence* is unlikely to forget this 8-foot-tall draped figure, its gaunt face darkened by age. Other members of the Graves family are also buried here, as indicated on a plaque engraved (sorry) with their names.

Eternal Silence reigns at Graceland Cemetery, which was established in 1860. The list of people interred there reads like a who's

This specter has a grave responsibility.

who of Chicago history. It's the final resting place for John Kinzie, Marshall Field, George Pullman, Potter and Bertha Palmer, Phillip Armour, Cyrus McCormick, and—believe it or not—Augustus Dickens, younger brother of Charles, who wrote *A Christmas Carol.* Unlike his older brother, Augustus is remembered by very few; in fact, until recently his Graceland plot was unmarked.

Graceland Cemetery is located at 4001 North Clark St. For more information, call (773) 525-1105 or visit www.gracelandcemetery.org.

Funk-o-Licious!

Kitsch'n On Roscoe

If you don't get the message from the picture of the dude in the Afro and purple shades on the side of the building, you'll get it once you step inside. That's when most people say, "Toto, I have a feeling we're not in the twenty-first century any more . . ."

Your first clue? Maybe the lava lamp or the electric curlers, or perhaps the poster of Jane Fonda as Barbarella or the stack of eight-track tapes. The more you look around, the further you sink into a retro-metro seventies funk-o-licious state—which is exactly where the owners of Kitsch'n On Roscoe are trying to put you. They would also settle for taking you back to the fifties or sixties. It's all good.

Jon Young and Helen Albert opened Kitsch'n On Roscoe in 1998, filling the restaurant with colorful Formica-topped tables and chrome chairs with vinyl seats. The couple gathered old board games, vintage toasters and lunchboxes, and innumerable other nostalgic items and put them on display. Beer can collections line the walls. A framed cover of *Sound Magazine* features the Partridge Family. The ladies room has a classic photo of Farrah Fawcett on the door, while a picture of Starsky and Hutch graces the men's room door.

The music of decades gone by rocks the place, and old-timey cartoons run continually on TV. While you wait for your food, you can amuse yourself with an Etch-a-Sketch, Mr. Potato Head, or Magic 8 Ball. Speaking of food, be prepared to dine on colorful Melmac

Put on those tinted shades—it's déjà vu
all over again at Kitsch'n On Roscoe!

plates, dinnerware molded from melamine resin. I recommend the
Cobb salad, which is served in a stainless steel bowl. The names of a
few of the menu items are loaded with nostalgia as well; for example,
Green Eggs and Ham, Not Your Mom's Meatloaf, Twinkie tiramisu,
and the ever-popular Tang martini.

Kitsch'n On Roscoe is located at 2005 West Roscoe St. For more
information, call (773) 248-7372 or visit www.kitschn.com.

The popular caramel-coated popcorn Cracker Jacks was invented in Chicago by F. W. Rueckheim in the late 1800s, and he started selling it under the name Cracker Jacks in 1896. In 1912 the company began to insert small toys into the packages.

Cubs-Woo!

Ronnie "Woo Woo" Wickers

Ronnie "Woo Woo" Wickers is one of a kind. He has been attending Cubs games at Wrigley Field since the 1940s, when he was just a lad. He has begged or borrowed his way into nearly every home game since the 1960s—even during the 1980s, when he was homeless.

The proud owner of around forty authentic Cubs jerseys with "Woo Woo" on the back, Wickers seldom wears anything else. During games he shrieks "Cubs-Woo! Cubs-Woo! Cubs-Woo!" or a variation thereof, such as "Zambrano-Woo!" He has such staying power that sportscaster Harry Caray dubbed him "Leather Lungs."

Over the years "Woo Woo" Wickers has become something of a celebrity, appearing on local and national television. His life was chronicled in a film by Paul Hoffman. In 2001 Wickers fulfilled a lifelong dream, leading the singing of "Take Me Out to the Ballgame" during the seventh-inning stretch of a Cubs game.

Those who know the self-appointed Cubs mascot describe him as kind-hearted, generous, and inspirational. Others use words like annoying and obnoxious. Now in his sixties, Wickers insists that he's simply being himself. "Look," he says, "people come and people go, life goes up and down, but the one constant is the Cubs."

For more information about the movie *Woo Life: One Life Saved by the Game of Baseball,* visit www.ronniewoowoo.com.

"A One . . . a Two . . . a Three . . . "

Harry Caray Statue

In my mind, I can still hear sportscaster Harry Caray's voice shouting his trademark exclamation—"HOLY COW!"—whenever something astonishing happened on the baseball field. I used to listen to Caray when he was a St. Louis Cardinals announcer in the 1950s and 1960s. Later on, he was a sportscaster for the Oakland Athletics, Chicago White Sox, and eventually the Chicago Cubs.

Holy cow! It's Harry Caray in bronze!

Caray passed away in 1998 at age eighty-four. When he was alive, his personality was larger than life. Now his statue looms large (7 feet tall) and in charge outside Wrigley Field. The heads of adoring Cubs fans rise up in front of him—or as the writers at RoadsideAmerica .com put it: "A bunch of tiny human heads seem to be bubbling out of his legs."

The statue's outstretched arms suggest that Caray is leading Cubs fans in one last rendition of "Take Me Out to the Ballgame." "Let me hear ya!" he would call out. "A one . . . a two . . . a three . . . " Unfortunately, the extended arms have proven too great a temptation for pranksters, who tend to hang dead goats from them—a reference to the "Billy Goat Curse" cast on the Cubs in 1945. Occasionally someone puts a can of beer in one of the statue's hands (usually a Budweiser, because Caray was their spokesman).

Sculpted by Omri Amrany and Lou Cella, the Caray statue is made of white bronze and sits on a 5-foot base of black granite. It's located outside Gate D at Wrigley Field, near the corners of Addison and Sheffield.

Give It Your Best Shot!
Reading Under the Influence

From a very young age, I knew I wanted to be a writer. Then I began reading about famous authors and was dismayed to discover that so many of them were smokers and alcoholics. I didn't drink alcohol or smoke and didn't have any desire to do either. How then, I wondered, could I be an author?

As an adult, I still don't smoke or drink much alcohol. Maybe that's why I'm not famous. But enough about me. Let's talk about something other than writing under the influence—like, for example, Reading Under the Influence, or RUI.

Developed by a group of Chicago writers in 2005, RUI meets on Wednesdays from 7:00 to 9:00 p.m. in the back room at Sheffield's Beer Garden and Backroom Barbecue Restaurant. The ambience

includes exposed brick, ductwork, and a glowing fireplace. Writers order a shot, toast the audience, down the shot, read a short piece of original work or an excerpt from a favorite book, then down another shot. The audience is encouraged to join in. (Question: Should synchronized drinking be an Olympic event?) In truth, at RUI the shot doesn't have to be alcohol. Apparently you can be a "real writer" without it.

Each meeting has a theme. In the past these have included Fighting Words, Dog Days, Call Me Daddy, Cubbie Blues, and Fool for Love. Although drinking is encouraged during the meeting, attendees often find themselves leaving their whiskey glass on the table as they listen, spellbound, to some darned good storytelling. Trivia contests follow the readings, along with drawings to win prizes such as gift certificates to local bookstores.

If you're interested in reading your work at RUI, you need to first attend at least one meeting. Then submit a hard copy of your work in person. Sheffield's is located at 3258 North Sheffield Ave. For more information, visit www.readingundertheinfluence.com.

Watch Out! He's Armed to the Teeth!
Always There Dental Care

Forget the Swamp Thing, Hannibal Lecter, and Pennywise the Clown. I've got something that will truly terrify you: a GIANT DENTIST! (Sound FX: Piercing scream. Fade to black.)

The enormous figure in white stands atop a sign reading ALWAYS THERE DENTAL CARE. Bwahahahaha! He's always there, ever vigilant, armed to the teeth with that colossal toothbrush.

Is he a superhero or supervillain? You make the call. Literally. Make the call: (773) 348-0565. But only if you want an appointment.

The reviews of Always There Dental Care at Yelp.com (yelp?!) seem quite positive in general. Apparently a significant number of people have been able to overcome their fear of the giant dentist. Some may find him attractive or even—dare I say it?—toothsome.

⋆ ⋆

Always There Dental Care is located in Lincoln Park at 2758 North Racine Ave. (between Diversey Parkway and Lincoln Avenue). For more information, call the number provided above or visit www .alwaystheredentalcare.net.

Taking dentistry to new heights, our hero guards the entrance of Always There Dental Care!

The Music Man

Audiences at Chicago Stadium between 1930 and 1974 enjoyed performances by Al Melgard, who played the gigantic stadium organ. Melgard had only nine fingers, having lost the index finger on his left hand in a carpentry accident. But that didn't stop the tall, thin, bald musician from playing the perfect song for any situation. At a political convention in 1932, he played "Happy Days Are Here Again" for Franklin D. Roosevelt. When a hockey coach complained about a call, Melgard played "Don't Cry, Joe." When a wrestler bumped his head and staggered, the notes of "Did You Ever See a Dream Walking?" reverberated through the stadium. Melgard passed away in 1977 at the age of eighty-eight.

Cows Gone Wild
A Public Art Exhibition

You've heard of having the world on a string, but what about having the world on a cow?

I'm talking about *Planet Chicowgo,* a work of art created by Illinois artist Lois Hrejsa for "Cows on Parade," a public art exhibition. *Planet Chicowgo* features a map of the world draped like a blanket over a cow's back. A yellow daisy is tucked festively behind one ear.

In 1999, inspired by a similar project in Switzerland, Chicago held a contest for local artists to produce designs for unadorned, life-size fiberglass cows. Local businesses could sponsor an artist-designed cow or purchase a blank cow to embellish themselves. More than 300 decorated cows were placed all over the city, labeled with names like *Out of Cowtowner, Cowch Potato, Moovie Cow, Dairy-Go-Round, Holy Cow!, Udder Gold, Carmen Moo-randa,* and *I Did Not Start the Chicago Fire.*

Mayor Richard Daley called Cows on Parade "the single largest and most successful event in the history of Chicago." The city's enthusiasm for the bevy of bovines was not surprising, given that Chicago's basketball team is the Bulls and "Holy Cow!" was a favorite exclamation of longtime Chicago Cubs announcer Harry Caray. And, of course, there was that little matter of Mrs. O'Leary's heifer and its wayward hoof, long suspected of starting the Great Fire of 1871.

After the exhibit, which lasted just over four months, most of the cows were sold through charity auctions or taken home by their patrons. A few remained on public display.

Planet Chicowgo can be found in the entrance hallway of the Lincoln Park Days Inn at 644 West Diversey Parkway. For more information about Cows on Parade Chicago, visit www.cowparade.net /press/346.

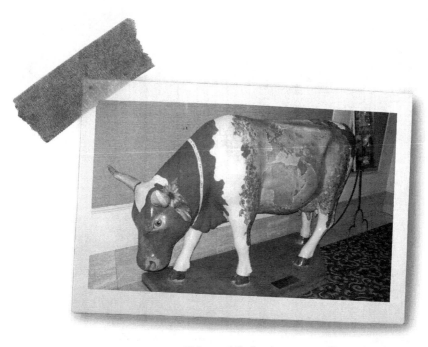

This worldly bovine graces the entrance hallway of the Lincoln Park Days Inn.

★ ★

Even Randy Might Like These!
Meatloaf Bakery

In one of my favorite scenes from the movie *A Christmas Story,* a little boy named Randy sits at the kitchen table, stirring, smashing, and mushing up the food on his plate. When his mother tells him not to play with his dinner, Randy mutters, "Meatloaf, shmeatloaf, double-beatloaf. I hate meatloaf."

Meatloaf Bakery presents the Mother Loaf.

A lot of kids (and quite a few adults) don't like meatloaf. If there's anything that can change their minds, it just might be Cynthia Kallile's meatloaf cupcakes.

Kallile left a career in corporate public relations to pursue what some would consider to be a very strange profession: baking meatloaf in the shape of a cupcake and topping it with mashed potato "frosting."

I used to make meatloaf with mashed potatoes on top, but Kallile has taken the idea to a whole new level. Her meatloaf cupcakes contain ground beef, pork, veal, chicken, turkey, salmon, or a combination. From that foundation she creates such masterpieces as:

- Yentl Lentil Loaf (lentils with brown rice, veggies, and cheese, topped with bell peppers, served with couscous)
- A Wing and a Prayer Loaf (ground chicken mixed with hot sauce, blue cheese, and celery, topped with blue cheese, served with ranch dressing)
- No Buns About It Burger Loaf (beef, bacon, cheddar, onions, mustard, ketchup, and pickles, topped with cheesy taters, served with special sauce)
- The Mother Loaf (beef, pork, and veal mixed with herbs and seasonings, topped with Yukon Smashers, served with demi-glace on the side). Yukon Smashers? Those are Yukon gold potatoes with plenty of butter and a smidge of sour cream.
- Kallile's Alaskan salmon concoction, called the Omega-3 Loaf, contains lemon, dill, and parsley. It's topped with wasabi mashed potatoes and served with lemon-dill yogurt.

"Meatloaf, shmeatloaf, double-beatloaf . . ." I LOVE meatloaf cupcakes!

Meatloaf Bakery is located at 2464 North Clark St. For more information, call (773) 698-6667 or visit www.themeatloafbakery.com.

★ ★

Statues and Flowers and Trees—Oh My!
Oz Park

"I'll get you, my pretty—and your little dog, too!"

I can't help it. That's my favorite line from the MGM movie *The Wizard of Oz,* probably because I played the role of the Wicked Witch of the West in a junior theater guild production of the play when I was a child. More recently, I went to see the musical *Wicked* in Chicago. Loved it!

However, if you insist, for this entry I'll focus on the characters who greet visitors to Oz Park. You won't find Her Wickedness there, but you can say hello to the Tin Man, Scarecrow, Cowardly Lion, and Dorothy and Toto.

Not only does Oz Park contain statues of these wonderful folks sculpted by artist John Kearney, areas within the park have names like "Dorothy's Playlot" and "Emerald Garden." (Interesting side note: "Dorothy's Playlot" is also a reference to Dorothy Melamerson, a retired local schoolteacher whose savings have paid for a number of park improvements.)

Oz Park was established in honor of Lyman Frank Baum (1856–1919), the author of *The Wonderful Wizard of Oz.* Born in New York, Baum settled in Chicago—several miles west of what is now the park—in 1891. Nine years later *The Wonderful Wizard of Oz,* a collaboration between Baum and Chicago cartoonist and poster designer W. W. Denslow, was published. Success was instant.

This thirteen-acre park has plenty of trees, flowers, and picnic tables (no deadly poppy fields, thank goodness). It's the perfect spot for walking a dog or strolling with your sweetheart, and an ideal place for munchkins to play. You'll also find recreational facilities such as basketball and tennis courts, a jogging path, and the Melamerson Athletic Field.

Oz Park is located at 2021 North Burling St. in the Lincoln Park neighborhood. For more information, call (312) 742-7898.

Oz Park's Scarecrow—if he only had a brain!

★ ★

Adding Insult to Injury

A distinct lack of compassion was shown in 1880 by a *Tribune* reporter who covered an attempted suicide. After quoting a suicide note that gave rejection by a woman as the reason for the attempt, the reporter commented: "The girl . . . probably gave him the mitten because of his homely physiognomy. That at least would furnish her a good excuse for so doing."

Survivor Chicago!
This Old House Lives On

The stately gray-blue Victorian house on North Cleveland Avenue doesn't call attention to itself. Granted, it's on a very nice lot in a very nice neighborhood, convenient to many Chicago attractions—but even so, it doesn't strike the casual observer as anything special. You're about to find out what the casual observer doesn't know about this house.

When the Great Chicago Fire blazed through town in 1871, the city's entire central business district was leveled. About $200 million worth of property was destroyed, and 100,000 people were left without homes. At least 300 people were killed. Those who survived took it upon themselves to rebuild the city, which they managed to do within two years.

Not every building that lay in the fire's path was destroyed. Some are still standing today, like the old water tower and pumping station (on North Michigan Avenue), St. Michael's Church in Old Town, and old St. Patrick's Church on Adams Street. Private buildings that survived include three houses in the Mid-North District: the Victorian at

This Victorian survived both the Great Fire of 1871 and the Extreme Makeover of the New Millennium.

2339 North Cleveland Ave., its twin next door at 2343 North Cleveland, and a third survivor at 2121 North Hudson.

You would never guess the distinguished history of the house at 2339 North Cleveland just by looking at it. You would also probably not guess that once you step inside, you'll be catapulted into the twenty-first century. There are a total of six bedrooms and six baths, plus a fully finished full basement. To quote from the real estate listing: "designer kitchen with adjoining great room, luxurious master suite (double sink and whirlpool in bath), lavish built-in cabinetry, beamed ceilings, hardwood floors, impeccable finishes."

This place really is a survivor—still standing after both a Great Fire and an Extreme Makeover!

Horror, Hauntings, and H. H. Holmes

Sightings on Sobieski Street

Herman Webster Mudgett (alias Dr. Henry Howard Holmes) murdered a large number of women at a hotel he operated in Chicago during the 1893 World's Columbian Exhibition. As you might expect, the former location of the "Murder Castle" in Englewood is reputed to be haunted. However, Chicago ghost hunter Adam Selzer has experienced weirder phenomena on Sobieski Street on the North Side, where Holmes operated a "glass bending factory." It's believed that the factory served as a body dump for Holmes's victims.

Goings-on include the sighting of a woman in a black dress and the sound of a woman weeping. On one visit to the spot, Selzer found three hawks with dead doves in their mouths. Then there's the flickering light. At first it appeared to be just a malfunctioning light. But Selzer noticed that on several occasions, every time he said "Holmes" or "Emily Van Tassel" (the name of one of the victims), the light would go off—or on, if it was already off. When I was there with Selzer on a ghost tour, the light did not "perform," but the overall vibe in the area was definitely creepy.

For more information on ghostly activities at the factory site and elsewhere in the Windy City, visit www.weirdchicago.com or http://weirdchicago.blogspot.com.

4

Northwest

The Northwest section *includes the area known as the Far Northwest Side, which contains the neighborhoods closest to O'Hare International Airport. Here you'll find large residential communities such as Avondale and the Polish Village, Irving Park, Forest Glen, Jefferson Park, Norwood Park, Edison Park, Edgebrook, Dunning, and Portage Park.*

The neighborhoods in the Northwest section are typically family-friendly and middle-class. It is said that the Chicago-style hot dogs in this region of the city are among the best. If you like Polish food, you can't improve on the Polish communities of Jackowo and Waclawowo (The Polish Village). Notice that Pulaski Road, which runs right through the area, was named for Casimir Pulaski, Polish soldier and Revolutionary War hero.

Residents of Irving Park have more options than most Chicagoans when it comes to transportation: trains, buses, the El, and the Kennedy Expressway all serve the neighborhood. Diverse architecture is one of the features of Cragin. Hermosa contains solid, family-oriented, working-class neighborhoods. If you're the outdoors type, you'll want to check out North Park Village Nature Center.

Forest Glen is one of the oldest neighborhoods in Chicago. The Pottawatomie Indians inhabited the area in the seventeenth century. Dunning, which was a remote prairie location in the 1800s, served as the location for Cook County's poor farm and asylum for the insane until around 1910.

Also included in this chapter are curiosities in Palatine and Niles.

Built on a Tilt
The Leaning Tower of Niles

Far away in an ancient and exotic land, there stands a stately tower that leans to one side. I'm not writing about that tower. I'm writing about a tower that sits in a Chicago suburb about 15 miles from downtown: the Leaning Tower of Niles.

Whereas the tilt of the Leaning Tower of Pisa was an accident (caused by the ground sinking at the time of its construction in the

Lean to the left, lean to the right, the Tower of Niles is quite a sight!

twelfth century), the Leaning Tower of Niles was deliberately built off-kilter (in 1934) to resemble its Italian cousin. The Niles tower is about half the size of the one in Pisa and doesn't lean nearly as far off plumb—but who's measuring? (Well, somebody clearly is. I'm told the Niles tower is 94 feet tall vs. 177 feet for the Pisa tower; the Niles version leans about 7 feet 4 inches off plumb vs. the original in Pisa, which boasts an alarming 15-foot tilt.)

According to a plaque at its base, the Leaning Tower of Niles was built to honor Italian scientist Galileo Galilei. Legend says that Galileo dropped things from the Pisa tower to prove that objects of different weights fall at the same speed. One wonders if science students at Niles schools are taken on field trips to duplicate the experiment allegedly performed by "the father of modern physics."

The Leaning Tower of Niles stands in front of the Tower YMCA at 6300 Touhy Ave. in Niles. For more information, call (847) 647-8222.

Who Let the Dawgs Out?!
Superdawg Drive-In

Who let the dawgs out? More important, who put them on the roof?

I'll tell you. A long time ago, when the earth was young—okay, it was 1948—Maurie and Flaurie Berman decided to open a roadside hot dog stand at the corner of Milwaukee, Devon, and Nagle in Chicago. They wanted to set their stand apart from the other hot dog stands popping up around the city, so Maurie designed an unusual 20-by-12-foot building. For the crowning touch, the Bermans topped their building with two 12-foot hot dog icons. One was clad in a Tarzan-style wrap; the other wore puffed sleeves, a ruffled skirt, and a sweet little chapeau. Their eyes blinked and winked like Christmas lights. Maurie and Flaurie then created a proprietary secret recipe for a creation they named Superdawg ("not a wiener—not a frankfurter—not a red hot . . . ").

Fast-forward to the here and now. The Superdawg icons have been refurbished (who among us has not?); the drive-in has been updated

No, you aren't hallucinating. There are two cos-
tumed hot dogs on top of that building.

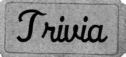

The original Oscar Mayer "Wienermobile"—an automobile shaped like a hot dog on a bun—was built in Chicago in 1936 by General Body Company.

with neon-studded canopies across the parking lot and a crisp new speaker system; and an indoor dining room was added in 1999. Menu items include not only the ultra-famous Superdawg and Super-fries, but the creatively named Whoopercheesie, Whoopskidawg, and Superchic sandwich.

But some things haven't changed. Superdawg continues to be family owned and operated. Customers can still order from their car and have a carhop deliver their order on a tray. It's silly. It's sassy. It's Superdawg!

Superdawg is located at 6363 North Milwaukee Ave. For more information, call (773) 763-0660 or visit www.superdawg.com.

Incredible Stuff!
American Science & Surplus

There are things you've always wanted that you don't know you want until you see them. These are the kinds of things you'll find at American Science & Surplus.

The last time I was there, I spotted treasures like Bat on a Stand (a skeleton of a bat), a Phony Phone (a radio/calendar/calculator that looks like a phone), Albert Einstein and Leonardo da Vinci action figures, and a Comparative Heart Set, featuring hearts from a fish, amphibian (frog), reptile (snake), bird (pigeon), and mammal (rabbit).

Don't have time to go there today? Check out the website! "Why lug a full-grown bullhorn around when you can get bullish sound from a much smaller bovine blaster?" the site asks concerning an item called the Calf Horn (or Mini-Mega-Phone). An ad for an adjustable spoon reads "Perfect for a moveable feast!" Another ad assures us: "Lash LaRue Lives! And Lash impersonators can now carry our authentic 6-foot bullwhip."

Wouldn't you love to know what the heck Das Hopper Popper is? Doesn't everyone need a Screeching Monkey Superhero? Haven't you always wanted an Accountant in a Jar? Where else can you get Puff the Magic AirZooka? And don't forget about lab supplies and equipment—you can never have too much of that!

The website offers a word of caution: "When a surplus item is gone, it is gone. So if you see something you love, best get it now since we may not have it tomorrow."

American Science & Surplus is located at 5316 North Milwaukee Ave. For more information, call (773) 763-0313) or visit www.sciplus.com.

The Midnight Bike Ride

Who on earth would go bike riding between midnight and dawn? As it turns out, thousands of people! Every year since 1989, participants in the L.A.T.E. (Long After Twilight Ends) Ride have been doing exactly that, en masse. The 25-mile route varies from year to year, but cyclists always begin and end at Buckingham Fountain in Grant Park. The event features live music, refreshments, sponsor booths, and a dazzling view of the sunrise over Lake Michigan. Proceeds benefit Friends of the Parks, a not-for-profit parks advocacy group. For more information, visit www.lateride.org.

Ghastly Ghoul or Gracious Granny?

Pilgrim Mother Sculpture

Like something from a scene in *Night of the Living Dead,* a hooded figure creeps through Bohemian National Cemetery. Stooped with age, aided by a walking stick, the figure slowly approaches a mausoleum. Is the creature living or dead? Where did it come from? Why is it here?

Dare to draw closer, and you'll realize that the larger-than-life-size figure is not moving, nor can it. It's sculpted out of bronze. And although it has been given the nicknames "Walking Death" and "The Grim Reaper," the statue was never intended to frighten anyone.

Is this a ghoul returning home after a hard night's work?
No, it's just the *Pilgrim Mother.*

★ ★

Trivia

Diehard Cubs fans can be buried at Bohemian National Cemetery near a red brick replica of one of the walls from Wrigley Field. The setting also incorporates a stained-glass replica of the Wrigley scoreboard as well as box seats, a dugout bench, and sod from the ball field. The section, called "Beyond the Vines," is advertised as "Eternal Luxury Skyboxes for Cubs Fans." For more information, visit http://beyondthevines.net.

In 1928 the Stejskal-Fuchal family commissioned Albin Polasek, a Czech-American sculptor, to design a piece to honor the mother of the family, who had recently passed away. Polasek's sculpture, *Pilgrim Mother,* was placed near the family burial chamber. The statue stands on a large stone slab. Two smaller slabs lie between the statue and the mausoleum, as if creating a path for the pilgrim to follow.

As decades pass, the *Pilgrim Mother* continues her never-ending, motionless journey, oblivious to the legends that have sprung up around her. According to one of these tales, anyone who peers under the hood to look at her face will see the manner of his own death. What I saw was an old woman's face with a peaceful, kind expression. Doesn't sound too bad to me.

Bohemian National Cemetery is located at 5255 North Pulaski Rd. The Stejskal-Fuchal mausoleum and *Pilgrim Mother* are in Section 18, in the northwest quadrant of the cemetery. For more information, call (773) 539-8442 or visit www.bohemiannationalcemeterychicago.org.

How Do You Lose a Cemetery?
Read Dunning Memorial Park

Any number of things can delay a construction project. Often problems can be attributed to human error or human nature. But in 1989 a project on the north side of Chicago was brought to a halt by human remains. I'm not talking about a few isolated corpses—I'm talking about the bodies of an estimated 38,000 people.

Imagine the surprise of sewer excavators when they discovered the mummified corpse of a man with an 1890s-style handlebar mustache and mutton-chop sideburns. Imagine uncovering baskets of bones. Imagine a city forgetting the existence of a cemetery that was used from about 1850 into the early 1900s.

Research revealed that the site being prepared for new construction was once the location of a poorhouse and an insane asylum known first as Dunning, then as Chicago State Hospital, and later as Chicago-Read Mental Health Center. The property also contained a tuberculosis hospital and a county cemetery.

As more bodies were discovered, religious leaders and residents of the neighborhood banded together to prevent further desecration of the cemetery. Their efforts eventually led to the creation of a memorial park on the spot where a developer had planned to build homes and condominiums.

The five-acre Read Dunning Memorial Park is a broad expanse of grass broken by a winding gravel path marked at intervals by concrete circles. With its stark signage, few trees, and one bench, the park has dignity but also conveys a sense of abject loneliness. It's impossible not to imagine the bleak, at times horrific, lives of many who are buried there, especially when you read the bronze plaques placed around the perimeter of the largest circle. They are inscribed "Unknown and Itinerant Poor of Cook County," "Cook County Poorhouse," "Orphaned and Abandoned Infants and Children," "The Sick and Infirm at Dunning," "The Cook County Insane Asylum," "Civil War Veterans," and "Unidentified Victims of the 1871 Chicago Fire."

Read Dunning Memorial Park lies at the west end of Belle Plaine Avenue, just beyond Narragansett Avenue and south of the Wright College North Campus. For more information, visit http://graveyards .com/IL/Cook/dunning or http://hiddentruths.northwestern.edu/ potters_field/disinters/county_potters.html.

Weep No More, My Lady
The Weeping Icon at St. Nicholas

When you enter St. Nicholas Albanian Orthodox Church at 2701 North Narragansett Ave., you experience a sense of history, of tradition, of something beyond the here and now. Rich browns, golds, and reds surround you. Everywhere you look, you see pictures of Jesus, his mother Mary, and various saints.

The icons are motionless and silent. No one expects them to exhibit human behavior. Yet on December 6, 1986, Father Philip Koufos noticed wet streaks on the icon of the Blessed Virgin Mary. He looked closer and saw that her eye was glistening as if filled with tears. Moisture could also be seen beneath her hand.

During the months that followed, this phenomenon drew hundreds

The weeping icon of St. Nicholas Albanian Orthodox Church

of thousands of people to the church. Eventually the moisture disappeared, but in 1988 moisture was again noticed on the icon. In 1995 another episode of what appeared to be weeping took place. No drips from the ceiling or leaking pipes were ever discovered.

Some say these events were miracles. Some call them "inexplicable signs of deep religious importance." Others refer to them simply as "phenomena." The icon at St. Nicholas wasn't the first (or last) icon or holy statue to behave in this manner. Many other instances have been reported in Chicago and all over the world. What does it mean?

Sweet Ride!
World's Largest Wagon

What's 27 feet long, 13 feet wide, 27 feet high, weighs 15,000 pounds, and seats 75 children comfortably? Read on.

Like so many wonderful people and things, the quintessential "little red wagon" was born in Chicago. During the 1920s Antonio

What 28-foot-tall child wouldn't love the
World's Largest Wagon™?

Pasin formed the Liberty Coaster Company, named after the Statue of Liberty. The company's first creation was the wooden Liberty Coaster wagon. Nearly a decade later, Pasin named his first steel wagon the Radio Flyer, honoring both the invention of the radio and the miracle of flight. At the 1933 Chicago World's Fair (A Century of Progress), a 45-foot-tall Coaster Boy wagon was one of the most popular exhibits.

In 1997, to celebrate its eightieth anniversary, Radio Flyer created a monument inspired by the World's Fair exhibit: a wagon measuring 27 feet long, 13 feet wide, and 27 feet high. A few other useful stats from the Radio Flyer Web site: The project required six tons of steel and a hundred gallons of secret-formula Radio Flyer Red paint. The wheels measure 8 feet in diameter and weigh 1,000 pounds each.

The World's Largest Wagon™ is located in Elmwood Park, at 6515 West Grand Ave. (Grand and Fullerton), next to the Radio Flyer factory. For more information, visit www.radioflyer.com/about/wlw.asp.

All Grim? Far from It!

Ahlgrim Acres

I think that this mortuary's name alone—Ahlgrim—qualifies it as a curiosity. ("All grim," get it?) Even curiouser is the 1958 Cadillac DeVille hearse the Ahlgrims use on special occasions. However, the most curious thing about Ahlgrim's Family Funeral Home can be found in the basement. Mwahahahaha!

Would you believe Ping-Pong, billiards, pinball machines, and video games? How about a nine-hole miniature golf course featuring a skull and bones, a replica of a graveyard, a haunted house, a castle with a guillotine entrance, and . . . wait for it . . . a coffin (with a one-stroke penalty if you bypass it)? Strategically placed road signs offer warnings such as DEAD END and DO NOT ENTER. And then there are the recordings of screams and spooky music that play continually.

Irreverent? Morbid?

Before you wag your finger at the Ahlgrims, be aware that Ahlgrim's Family Funeral Home—founded in Chicago in 1892 as Ahlgrim

The community room in the basement of Ahlgrim's Family
Funeral Home features a miniature golf course.
DOUGLAS R. AHLGRIM

Undertakers—has a long tradition of very high standards and a
respected name in the funeral industry. The community room is only
available when there are no funerals or visitations in progress. Doug
Ahlgrim—a fourth-generation funeral director—is quick to point out
that, contrary to rumors floating around the Internet, the funeral
home does not offer miniature golf as part of a funeral package.

The community room now known as Ahlgrim Acres was made
accessible to the public in 1965. It is continually being updated and
improved. At the same time, around 300 funerals are held at Ahlgrim's each year. It's obvious that permitting fun and games in the
basement hasn't interfered with the family's ability to provide funeral
services with dignity and compassion.

Ahlgrim Acres is located at 201 North Northwest Hwy. in Palatine,
a northwestern residential suburb of Chicago. For more information,
call (847) 358-7411 or visit www.ahlgrimffs.com.

5

West Side

Chicago's West Side *contains Austin, the city's largest neighborhood, both in size and in population. Originally an upscale suburb, Austin has gone through some rough times but is now experiencing revitalization.*

Humboldt Park is a working-class neighborhood and cultural strong-hold of Chicago's Puerto Rican community. The neighborhood hosts an annual Puerto Rican Peoples Parade and Puerto Rican Pride festival.

Wicker Park in West Town is a haven for the arts and counterculture, with an emphasis on performance art and theater. Historically popu-lated by older citizens of Eastern European ethnicity, Ukrainian Village contains the Ukrainian Institute of Modern Art, the Ukrainian National Museum, and the Ukrainian Cultural Center.

East Garfield Park, named one of America's most "up and coming neighborhoods" in a 2007 issue of Business Week, *contains one of the city's hidden gems: the Garfield Park Conservatory, filled with plants, flowers, waterfalls, and koi ponds. West Garfield Park is a work in prog-ress, as organizations strive to rehabilitate housing and rekindle a sense of pride in the neighborhood.*

Once a haven for Greek immigrants, Greektown features numerous restaurants, a cultural museum, and annual festivities. Back in 1968, Chicago's Greektown introduced Americans to gyros and saganaki (flaming cheese). Chicago's Greek Independence Day Parade typically takes place in April.

Between June and October, locals flock to the Lawndale Chicago

Farmers Market. South Lawndale is the heart of Chicago's Mexican community. North Lawndale suffered from violent crime during the 1970s and 1980s, but development programs are having an impact.

Pilsen was named after Plzen, the fourth-largest city in what is now the Czech Republic. Inhabited by Czech immigrants in the late nineteenth century, Pilsen is Chicago's largest Latino community today. Although poverty and related social problems are an ongoing concern, Pilsen's residents are committed to building a better neighborhood, one that reflects the community's rich cultural and organizational base.

Also included in this chapter are curiosities located in Hillside, Forest Park, Oak Park, and Brookfield.

Talk About Well Preserved!

Julia Buccola Petta, the Italian Bride

It's tragic to lose a child, and even more tragic to lose both a child and a grandchild at the same time. Filomena Buccola's grief over the death of her twenty-nine-year-old daughter, Julia, in childbirth in 1921 was intense and overwhelming. But the dreams that followed the burial were even more powerful.

In Filomena's dreams, her daughter repeatedly asked her to open her grave. Filomena became convinced that Julia was still alive. For six long years, Filomena begged authorities to exhume the remains. Finally, in 1927, a local priest approved her request and permission was granted.

No, Julia was not alive. However, to the amazement of everyone present at the casket opening, the lovely young woman's remains were intact, as beautiful as the day she was buried. After six years in the ground, the casket was muddy and somewhat rotted, but Julia's body was flawless—no evidence of decay, decomposition, or discoloration.

Today, a photograph inserted into the monument testifies to this startling phenomenon. The monument itself—called *The Italian*

Bride—shows Julia in her wedding gown, holding a bouquet of roses. A reproduction of her wedding photo also appears on the front of the monument.

It is said that an uncorrupted body signifies that the person is a saint. To learn more, you could hang around the cemetery and ask the apparition of a woman in a white dress that occasionally appears near Julia's grave.

Imagine looking this good after six years in the ground! Julia Buccola Petta did.

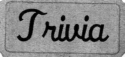

The World's Columbian Exposition, held in Chicago in 1893, introduced many well-known products to consumers, including Aunt Jemima Syrup, diet carbonated soda, Shredded Wheat, Juicy Fruit gum, Cream of Wheat, Pabst beer, and Cracker Jacks.

Julia Buccola Petta's grave and monument are located in Section A (on Harrison Street) at Mount Carmel Cemetery, 1400 South Wolf Rd., Hillside. Call (708) 449-8300 or visit www.catholiccemeteries chicago.org.

The Family That Stays Together . . .

Di Salvo Monument

We all know that family gatherings can be a bit strange. Sometimes everybody sits around staring at everybody else in stony silence. Then the whole group rotates 90 degrees to face a different direction.

What? You've never been at a family gathering like that? Consider yourself lucky. The Di Salvos are stuck in one of those gatherings for all eternity—or at least for as long as their marble sculpture lasts.

There they stand—with the exception of Mama Rosa Di Salvo, who sits—destined to forever hold their peace while life goes on around them. Well, not all that much life, given that they're in a cemetery.

A young man stands behind Mama. Two women and a young girl stand in front of her. Mama's hand is on a book that rests on a stone railing covered with a vine, and the young girl also holds a book. The level of detail in the family's clothing is remarkable, in a style suggesting the late 1800s. Perhaps the sculpture was based on a family photograph from that era.

As if an elaborate marble sculpture were not enough, the

monument rotates 360 degrees on a marble dais, like a turntable. Maybe the sculptor thought the Di Salvos would be bored gazing at the same view day after day and decided to make it possible for them to have a change of scenery from time to time.

The marker identifies the parents of the family as Angelo (1869–1943) and Rosa (1872–1927) Di Salvo. Photographs of the two are also mounted on the stone. At the base of the sculpture are the words LAROSA and FLORENCE 1891. This most likely refers to the stone carver and where and when the monument was carved, although some have interpreted "Florence" as the name of a family member.

The Di Salvo monument is located in Section 19 of Mount Carmel Cemetery at 1400 South Wolf Rd. in the Chicago suburb of Hillside. For more information, call (708) 449-8300 or visit www.catholic cemeterieschicago.org.

Together forever: the Di Salvo family

Gone but Not Forgotten
Al Capone's Grave

Called the "Big Fellow" by his friends, Al "Scarface" Capone still looms large as the most notorious organized crime kingpin in American history.

Born in New York, Alphonse Capone arrived in Chicago in 1919 at age twenty. By 1927 he was so well known that tour buses regularly included his headquarters in their rounds. Although he died in 1947, television shows and movies have kept his memory alive. *The Untouchables,* a popular TV series that aired from 1959 to 1963,

The grave of notorious gangster Al Capone
is marked by a simple stone slab.

★ ★

pitted Capone (played by Neville Brand) against federal agent Eliot Ness (Robert Stack). Ness was the hero of the show, but Capone stole more than his share of scenes.

One might say that Capone is "in good company" (or at least appropriate company) in Mount Carmel Cemetery. Some of the other criminals and gangland members interred there are Dion O'Banion, Hymie Weiss, "Machine Gun Jack" McGurn, Frank "The Enforcer" Nitti, Antonio "The Scourge" Lombardo, and Sam "Mooney" Giancana. And, of course, Capone is surrounded by family, including brothers Ralph ("Bottles") and Salvatore ("Frank").

Visitors to Capone's grave sometimes leave tokens of their esteem such as flowers, money, whiskey, cigars, and plastic replicas of guns. Even if you aren't a fan, standing there staring down at the rectangular slab inscribed ALPHONSE CAPONE 1899–1947 can be a memorable experience. The man who once said "They've hung everything on me except the Chicago fire" is gone but not forgotten.

Al Capone's grave is located in Section 35 in Mount Carmel Cemetery, 1400 South Wolf Rd., Hillside. Enter the cemetery off of Roosevelt Road and take the first turn to the right. For more information, call (708) 449-8300 or visit www.catholiccemeterieschicago.org.

Nothing Doing

It may be hard to imagine in a city like Chicago, but there was at least one morning in 1854 when crime took a holiday. A report in the *Tribune* read: "There was nothing doing on Monday morning—a very unusual circumstance in the annals of our Police Court."

But Was It Covered by Her Health Insurance Plan?

Maggie's Extreme Makeover

What should you do about cracked skin, a severe weight problem, bad teeth, brittle hair, and a short attention span?

At age forty-three, Maggie, an orangutan living at the Brookfield Zoo, stood 3 feet tall and weighed nearly 200 hundred pounds. She had severe headaches, dry skin, intestinal problems, and respiratory

MAGGIE'S MAKEOVER

Meet Maggie (born in July of 1961), an orangutan who recently underwent an "extreme makeover."

BEFORE

In August 2003, Maggie began medication for an underactive thyroid gland. Since then, her dry skin, brittle hair, inactivity, nasal discharge, constipation, excessive snoring, and flatulence have greatly improved. Plus, she has gone down from 220 to 130 pounds.

AFTER

Maggie's team included Brookfield Zoo veterinarians, nutritionists, and keepers, as well as experts from the University of Chicago and the Mayo Clinic in Rochester, Minnesota.

Beautiful lady!
WENDY MCCLURE

problems. Her auburn hair was brittle and dull. Worst of all, she had been suffering from these troubles all her life.

Then, in 2003, newly available tests revealed that she had hypothyroidism. Once she was on medication, Maggie's condition improved dramatically. Dietary changes had not helped in the past, but now they did. She lost ninety pounds, and her other health issues cleared up. People began to contact the zoo, asking if the medication Maggie received would work for them (the answer was yes!).

At the end of 2004, a veterinarian was quoted as saying he hoped the treatment would give Maggie "a few more years." Six years after that, she's still around, sharing the orangutan habitat with several others of her kind, including a little one named Kekasih, born in 2008 to an orangutan named Sophia.

Where Else but eBay?

You can get anything you want on eBay, including a demented Twilight Zone rabbit, a tooth that resembles the Virgin Mary, and a haunted barber chair. In 2004 Chicago auctioned off pieces of itself on eBay to raise money for the arts. Dubbed the Great Chicago Fire Sale, the auction accepted bids on things like the opportunity to dye the Chicago River green on St. Patrick's Day, dinner for ten with television broadcaster Bill Kurtis (accompanied by a documentary about the winning bidder's life), the chance to turn on Buckingham Fountain, and a 1960s Playboy Bunny costume.

Brookfield Zoo is located at 3300 Golf Rd. in Brookfield. For more information, call (708) 485-2200 or visit www.czs.org/czs/Brookfield /Zoo-Home.

Clowning Around in the Cemetery

Showmen's Rest

Combine clowns and graveyards, and what do you get (besides a novel by Stephen King)? If you're in Chicago, you get Showmen's Rest, a 750-plot section of Woodlawn Cemetery that serves as the final resting place for circus folk.

Professional clown Susan Hooper poses with an elephant monument at Showmen's Rest during International Clown Week.
ROSE M. HOOPER

Created by Buffalo Bill Cody and the Showmen's League of America in 1913, Showmen's Rest is surrounded by five elephant monuments, trunks lowered in mourning. Buried here are around sixty employees of the Hagenbeck-Wallace Circus who died in a train wreck near Hammond, Indiana, in 1918. The identity of many of the victims was unknown. Markers bear such names as "Smiley," "Baldy," and "Unknown Female No. 43."

Most of the left half of the Showmen's plot contains victims of the 1918 wreck. The other half is used for burials of other circus performers, up to the present day.

On the first Sunday of August each year, during International Clown Week (established in 1971 by none other than president Richard Nixon), Showmen's Rest is alive with clowns in full costume. At this public event, refreshments are served and kids of all ages are entertained with games, balloons, face painting, magicians, and jugglers.

Woodlawn Cemetery is located at 7750 Cermak Rd. (at the intersection of Cermak Road and Des Plaines Avenue) in Forest Park. For more information about the cemetery, call (708) 442-8500. For information about International Clown Week and the Showmen's Rest annual event, visit www.internationalclownweek.org and http://performforthe love.com/showmensrest.

Concrete Evidence of Success

Unity Temple

It's something to strive for: to be over one hundred years old and still doing what you were designed to do, even after breaking nearly every rule from the beginning.

Welcome to Unity Temple. Designed by renowned architect Frank Lloyd Wright and built between 1906 and 1908, Unity Temple is one of the earliest public buildings constructed of concrete—poured in place and left exposed. As if that weren't unusual enough, Wright chose a cubist design for the church, with no steeple, no front entrance, and sixteen separate flat roofs.

One can imagine members of the religious architecture establishment collapsing into their mahogany wingback chairs, whereupon they were offered smelling salts and a glass of water.

To prevent the facade from being "severely simple," Wright added a continuous plane of windows and ornamented columns. Not only that, the interior more than makes up for the exterior's limited warmth. Wright described the inside of the temple as his "jewel box," and it is widely viewed as one of the world's most inspiring sacred spaces.

Now structurally compromised, Unity Temple is undergoing extensive renovation—yet it continues to serve its original purpose as a location for Unitarian Universalist worship services, religious education programs, and other activities.

Unity Temple is located at 875 Lake St. in Oak Park. For more information or to schedule a tour, call (708) 383-8873 or visit www .oprf.com/unity.

Oh, Do You Know the Muffler Man?
Mr. Bendo

As storm clouds amass overhead, Bendo the Mighty looms over the horizon. Zeus-like, he raises a lightning bolt and . . . oh, wait. That's not a lightning bolt in his hand. Let me try again.

Like the Guardian Angel of mechanics conferring a blessing, Mr. Bendo stands atop an auto body shop, arm outstretched. Okay, that's way too dramatic. He's a Muffler Man. I need to just calm down.

As it turns out, Mr. Bendo is a chain of muffler shops, so this extra-large guy can be found not only in Illinois but also in Indiana and South Dakota, and maybe other places. Apparently he doesn't always wield an iron bar, leaving people to speculate about whether he is giving some sort of "heil, Hitler" salute or simply raising his hand to ask to go to the bathroom. Other versions have him holding one hand palm up and one palm down in front of him.

Bendo the Magnificent looms like a
Colossus atop the auto body shop!

If you really love giant people statues, check out Debra Jane Selt-
zer's Web site at www.agilitynut.com/giants/main.html. Mr. Bendo is
located at 3940 West Grand Ave.

All Dolled Up

JoJo's Closet (and More!)

From the outside, the Flat Iron Arts Building looks like any other three-story, triangular, terracotta-clad brick, Greek Revival–style building. Okay, maybe there aren't that many of those around. I'll concede that the exterior is unusual, but just wait until you go inside.

I happened to encounter JoJo of JoJo's Closet the last time I was in the Flat Iron Arts Building. Photo op!

★ ★

Trivia

Walt Disney was born in Chicago in 1901, in a frame cottage on North Tripp Avenue. Disney lived there until the age of four, when his family moved to Missouri. Returning to Chicago in 1917, the Disneys settled on the Near West Side. Walt Disney was a senior at McKinley High School and attended classes at the Academy of Fine Arts.

Be prepared for vaulted tin ceilings, turn-of-the-century oak trim on the stairwells, and a labyrinth of hallways that lead you into a world where art doesn't just imitate life, it is life. The building is home to more than thirty resident artists, studios, and galleries. Here you'll find sculptures, oil paintings, watercolors, puppets, collages, comic book art—just about anything you can imagine.

Case in point: JoJo's Closet. Picture a bright, lime green wrought-iron door with lightbulbs all around it. Above the door is a large poster of Jo-Jo the Dog-Faced Boy of circus sideshow fame. Artist JoJo Baby opens the door and you're suddenly looking into a world literally filled with bizarre dolls and puppets of all sizes. A man of many talents, JoJo is not only a doll-maker but a well-known Chicago club personality and hair sculptor (among his past clients: former Chicago Bulls star Dennis Rodman).

On the first Friday of each month from 6:00 to 10:00 p.m., the artists in the Flat Iron Arts Building open their living spaces and studios to the public. The event features guest artists, impromptu performances, and refreshments.

The Flat Iron Arts Building is located at 1579 North Milwaukee Ave. For more information about the building, call (312) 335-3000 or visit

✦ ✦

http://theflatironchicago.com. For more information about JoJo Baby, visit www.jojochicago.com.

Looking for Quirky Crafts?
Renegade Handmade

Let's say you're looking for something unusual in a gift—for example, a brooch shaped like an artichoke, a Braille poetry scarf, a Fudgsicle Bath Fizzle, or a recycled seat belt camera strap. Or maybe you've always wished you had a naked mole rat night light, an angry toast pocket friend, or baby burp cloths labeled "puke," "spew," and "hurl."

Abbey Hambright's finger puppets (Ira Glass, Willie Nelson, Bob Ross) are best sellers at Renegade Handmade.
ABBEY HAMBRIGHT

★ ★

You won't find these items at major department stores, but don't despair! There's a charming little shop in Chicago's Wicker Park neighborhood that offers the unique, often startling work of over 300 artists. It's called Renegade Handmade.

The store was created as an extension of the Renegade Craft Fair, an annual event organized by crafter Susie Daly and a childhood friend. The pair were discussing fairs to apply to, and the friend remarked, "I wish there was just a 'renegade' craft fair out there." Daly suggested they start their own.

The first fair was held in Chicago in 2003. Daly now coordinates similar fairs in other large cities such as New York, Los Angeles, and San Francisco. In 2007 Daly and her associates set up shop on Division Street. The merchandise can be described as offbeat, ironic, edgy, humorous, subversive, funky, and—above all—highly original. Whether you're looking for a Willy Nelson finger puppet or a tote bag

Way to Go, Willie!

If you're a Stevie Ray Vaughan fan, you may have heard of "Willie the Wimp and his Cadillac coffin." Vaughn didn't make that up. The deceased in question was the very real Willie Stokes Jr. During the 1970s and early '80s, Stokes and his father built a reputation as Chicago bad guys by beating people up and selling drugs. They also got rich. When Junior (aka "Willie the Wimp") was murdered in 1984, his father spared no expense. Junior, dressed in a red velvet suit and pearl gray hat, was buried in a "casketmobile" with a Cadillac grill, blinking headlights, and whitewall tires.

made from a flour sack, you'll find it at Renegade Handmade or at the Renegade Craft Fair.

Renegade Handmade is located at 1924 West Division St. For more information, call (773) 227-2707 or visit www.renegadehand made.com. For information about the Renegade Craft Fair, visit www .renegadecraft.com.

Dedicated to the Dogs
S*** Fountain

Get ready, because this entry is going to be a fountain of information about—what else?—fountains. Chicago has a marvelous selection of fountains.

For example, there is Buckingham Fountain, made of pink marble and embellished with four bronze seahorses. Crown Fountain features two facing 50-foot glass-block towers that project video of Chicago faces. Centennial Fountain shoots a majestic arc of water across the Chicago River. There are lovely fountains on North LaSalle and at Nichols Park and Lakeshore East Park.

A fountain can cool your body on a hot afternoon, delight your eyes with its artistic design, or provide a relaxing interlude in the middle of a hectic day. Well, a lot of them can. Then there's the fountain on North Wolcott Avenue at West Augusta Boulevard.

This fountain sits on private property atop a 3-foot-high column made of concrete and sandstone. So far, so good. It was crafted in bronze by internationally known Chicago artist Jerzy S. Kenar. That's a definite "plus." Kenar created the holy water font at Loyola University's Madonna della Strada Chapel and the granite Black History Fountain at Renaissance Park on Chicago's South Side.

The thing is, this fountain is . . . um . . . unique (some would say not in a good way). Kenar, who unveiled his creation at a Fourth of July party in 2005, dedicated it to all the dogs in the neighborhood. One look at it, and you understand why. It's a larger-than-life replica of what dogs have been depositing on lawns for centuries. These days, owners are expected to clean up after their canines, but not all of them bother.

★ ★

The Fountain Whose Name Shall Not Be
Mentioned in Polite Company

A work of art can inspire, motivate, and stir the soul. Or not. In this case, Kenar merely hopes that his fountain will encourage people to bring a pooper scooper with them when they walk their dog.

Reactions have been mixed. A member of the garden club chided Kenar for undermining efforts to beautify the neighborhood. She later admitted that after she saw the fountain, she laughed all the way home.

The fountain—whose name shall not be mentioned in polite company—is located at 1001 North Wolcott Ave.

Food So Good, It's Criminal!

Felony Franks

It's nice when a curiosity provides me with the perfect title. I can't improve on the Felony Franks slogan as a heading for this entry: "Food so good, it's criminal!"

Chicagoans disagree about what's criminal about this hot dog stand: the extreme tastiness of the food or the owner's tasteless choice of a prison theme. The reason for the theme becomes clear

Do you want Freedom Fries with that?

★ ★

when you find out that Jim Andrews, the owner of Felony Franks, hires ex-convicts to staff the place. Andrews says his purpose is to give criminals who've served their time a second chance to be productive members of society. To that end, he also created the Rescue Foundation in 2003 to help ex-offenders, and he has hired them at his local paper company for years.

Felony Franks applies the prison motif to all aspects of its operation. The restaurant, a cramped space with no seating, is framed by cinder-block walls. The logo features a hot dog in prison stripes peering through jail bars. Menu items include the Misdemeanor Wiener, Pardon Polish, Chain Gang Chili Dog, and Probation Burgers. Sides like coleslaw and relish are called "accomplices." A sign offers customers the Felony Franks equivalent of their Miranda rights, beginning with: "You have the right to remain hungry."

Those who object loudest to what Andrews has done aren't against his employing ex-offenders. They just think the theme is detrimental to a neighborhood that is striving to improve itself and stigmatizes ex-convicts by focusing attention on that part of their lives, making it harder for them to blend back into society.

I wish I could report on the quality of food at Felony Franks, but the place was so crowded when I stopped by that I ended up going somewhere else for lunch. What? Is that a crime? So sue me!

Felony Franks is located at 229 Western Ave. (between Adams Street and Lake Street). For more information, call (312) 243-0505.

Miracle on Roosevelt Road
Holy Family Church

The strangest thing about Holy Family Church is that it's still standing. Like the proverbial cat, it appears to have more than one life.

It was "born" in 1857, when it was founded by Father Arnold Damen, a well-known Jesuit priest. Back then the spot on which it was built was on the outskirts of town. The Victorian Gothic-style church was dubbed "a European cathedral on the Illinois prairie."

Holy Family Church survived the Great Fire, which
started six blocks away at the O'Leary barn.

"Tough Guy"

An article in the *Chicago Daily Tribune* on August 18, 1880, told of S. R. Nublett, who lived at a boardinghouse at 177 West Ohio St. Nublett often bragged about how he had brutally murdered a man in Kentucky. His fellow residents treated him with deference and gave him lots of space, which was no doubt exactly what he wanted.

To Nublett's dismay, an "overofficious" person called the local police, who "speedily arrested Nublett and jailed him as a criminal." A telegram to Kentucky elicited the information that no such murder had occurred. Released from police custody, Nublett was described as "anxiously inquiring why he was treated thus."

Fast-forward fourteen years to 1871. About half a mile from the church stood a modest home and barn belonging to church members Patrick and Catherine O'Leary. The O'Leary barn, as you may recall, is believed to be the place where the Great Chicago Fire started. Yes, this is a setup. Are you ready?

According to legend, Father Damen was in New York when he received a telegram notifying him that the church was in peril. He invoked Our Lady of Perpetual Help to save the building, promising that if the church were spared, he would keep seven candles burning forever before Our Lady's statue. The wind carried the flames in a different direction (even the O'Leary house survived), and the church was unharmed.

This is why, when you visit Holy Family Church, you will see a shrine featuring seven candles before an image of the Virgin Mary

(Our Lady of Perpetual Help). Father Damen was as good as his word, and those who came after him continued to honor the promise.

The church nearly "lost its life" on two other occasions over the years—once because of financial problems and once because of a fire in the basement. Yet this "Miracle on Roosevelt Road" remains. It's the second-oldest church in Chicago.

Holy Family Church is located at 1080 West Roosevelt Rd. For more information, call (312) 492-8442 or visit www.holyfamilychicago.org.

Look Up an Old Flame
Pillar of Fire

Okay, let's just settle this once and for all: The Great Chicago Fire of 1871 was not caused by Mrs. O'Leary's cow kicking over a lantern. Catherine O'Leary always claimed she and her cow were innocent, and in 1997—on the 126th anniversary of the fire—historians and an O'Leary descendant convinced the city's Committee on Police and Fire to clear the infamous pair. There. I'm glad that's all straightened out. What's not in dispute is that the Great Chicago Fire did indeed occur on a warm, windy night in October 1871. It started near or in the O'Leary barn and raged for more than thirty hours before finally dying out. Much of downtown Chicago and surrounding areas were reduced to ruins. Amazingly, within two years Chicago was completely rebuilt. In physical terms, the new city was far superior to the old one—so much so that Chicago actually celebrated the two-year anniversary of the fire in 1873.

Maybe that's why it's called the "Great" Fire. No? But it could be why the bronze sculpture commemorating the event has a sort of triumphant look about it. *Pillar of Fire*'s stylized flames reach upward, reminding us not only of the beauty and danger of fire, but the resilience and vision of those who survived the disaster.

Designed by sculptor Egon Weiner, an instructor at the Art Institute from 1945 to 1971, *Pillar of Fire* stands where the fire is believed to have started. You have to love the fact that the Chicago Fire Academy

Flames mark the spot where the Great Fire
started. (And no, the cow didn't do it.)

training facility is located on the same infamous spot. The 33-foot *Pillar of Fire* monument was completed in 1961, and the site was designated as a Chicago Landmark in 1971.

Pillar of Fire is located at 558 West De Koven St. For more information, call (312) 747-7238 or visit www.cpfta.com.

Growing Up Chocolate: Family Business Spans Four Generations
Blommer Chocolate Company

The air around the Blommer Chocolate Company smells even better than what you might expect. The minute you walk into their air space, you are transported in your mind to a land of hot cocoa, warm brownies, devil's food cake, fudge, and chocolate chip cookies. How do I love thee, chocolate? Let me count the ways: milk chocolate, sweet chocolate, semisweet or bittersweet chocolate, unsweetened or baking chocolate, white chocolate, cocoa . . .

The Blommer Chocolate Company has been flavoring the air northwest of the Loop since 1939, when it was founded by Blommer brothers Henry, Al, and Bernard. The business, which is still family-run, has grown to be one of the largest chocolate manufacturers in North America.

In the public store, you'll find heaven by the pound: milk and dark chocolate; chocolate-covered pretzels, raisins, cashews, bananas, and cherries; cordials; and more. While you're there, be sure to pick up some baking chocolate in the form of chips, discs, chunks, or bars.

As delightful as I find it to be surrounded by the aroma of warm chocolate, I don't know how I would feel if I had to spend a lot of time within smelling distance of this place. That over-the-top sensation might quickly cross the line from ecstasy to agony—or at least to nausea. I can't even imagine what it would be like to work there.

The Blommer Chocolate Company is located at 600 West Kinzie St. For more information, call (312) 226-7700 or visit www.blommer.com.

141

Pageantry, Gadgetry, Acrobatics, Ephemera!
Redmoon Theater

Puppeteers manipulate characters and objects in a "cabinet of curiosities." Villains and heroes create a drama inside a toy theater. Characters interact with each other as 14-foot-tall moveable walls continually transform into different rooms.

In case you haven't noticed, this is not your father's theater experience! Come to think of it, it's probably not even *your* theater experience unless you have experienced Redmoon Theater.

Founded in 1990, Redmoon describes its performance style as "equal parts pageantry, gadgetry, acrobatics, and ephemera." Redmoon Theater is "committed to creating unexpected theater in unexpected locations," locations that have included the Jackson Park Lagoon, the White House in Washington, D.C., and Redmoon Central, a huge (18,500-square-foot) warehouse on the west side of Chicago.

I visited Redmoon Central while the cast and crew were setting the stage for *The Winter Pageant,* an annual family event that showcases the progression of the seasons and celebrates the return of spring. I was mesmerized by the props, contraptions, and devices that surrounded me in the vast, raw warehouse. And that was before anybody even started performing!

Once under way, *The Winter Pageant* took the audience on a mad caper through the seasons via a series of surrealistic scenes that incorporated human clouds, a big blue car filled with bakers carrying cakes and pies, white rice-paper cranes lit from within, deep-sea divers with soap-bubble-generating tanks on their backs, and a pirate ship manned by a trio of hearty swashbucklers singing a sea chantey about investing in the stock market.

Reviewers and audience members have described Redmoon performances as fresh, vigorous, evocative, intellectually stimulating, otherworldly, spellbinding, eerie, absurd, ethereal, funny, disturbing, truly inventive, inspiring, wacky, ridiculously original, and whimsical. I could go on, but I won't. You'll just have to see it for yourself!

Redmoon Theater productions feature complex contraptions like this one. Somewhere in there is a drum kit.

The Redmoon Theater warehouse (Redmoon Central) is located at 1463 West Hubbard St. For more information, call (312) 850-8440 or visit http://redmoon.org.

The abbreviation ORD for Chicago's O'Hare airport comes from the original name Orchard Field. O'Hare International Airport was named in honor of Lieutenant Commander Edward H. "Butch" O'Hare.

In the Realms of the Unreal
Intuit: The Center for Intuitive and Outsider Art

It isn't the sort of thing you expect to see when you visit an art museum, but there it is: a one-room apartment, complete with a cast-iron fireplace, chandelier, fragments of wallpaper, furniture, devotional statues, and stacks upon piles of books, magazines, art supplies, and trash from the streets.

But Intuit is no ordinary art museum. It's devoted to the work of "artists who demonstrate little influence from the mainstream art world and who seem instead motivated by their unique personal visions." Enter Henry Darger, whose apartment in Lincoln Park (where he lived from 1930 until shortly before his death in 1973) has been turned into an exhibit to accompany displays of his art.

Darger was what many would describe as an "odd duck." Born in Chicago in 1892, he was placed in an asylum for feeble-minded children at age thirteen. He ran away three years later. As an adult he was employed at various menial jobs, then retired due to illness in 1963. His magnum opus—titled *In the Realms of the Unreal*—consists of 19,000 pages of legal-size paper filled with single-spaced typing, supplemented by several hundred watercolor paintings. When Darger died, the contents of his apartment, along with his personal archives, were donated to Intuit by his landlords, Nathan and Kiyoko Lerner.

Further details about Darger, now considered one of the most prominent artists of the twentieth century, can be found through

Henry Darger's apartment, as re-created by Intuit,
offers a glimpse into a most curious mind and life.

many sources. What piques my curiosity for the purposes of this book
is not only Darger as an individual, but the reconstruction of his one-
room apartment, which served as both living quarters and studio.

It's important to note that there was no effort to replicate the
room exactly. What Intuit has done is to "evoke the intimate scale
and dense setting" in which Darger spent forty years. One can only
stare and marvel at this glimpse into the life of a most unusual man.

Intuit is located at 756 North Milwaukee Ave. For more information, call (312) 243-9088 or visit www.art.org.

A Sport That Gets Right to the Point

Sweeping and Swiping with the CSG

Sports are big in Chicago. You name it, they've got it: football, basketball, baseball, hockey, soccer, and that other sport. You know, the one where people slash, parry, lunge, sweep, swipe, and cut—and that's just while they're competing for a parking place at the event!

But seriously, the sport I'm talking about is swordplay. Swordplay? Yes, swordplay! It's all about slashing, lunging, swiping—and lots of other things you can do with a sword. There is also a fair amount of grappling involved.

Twice a week about two dozen or so students and instructors gather at the Chicago Park District's Pulaski Park field house on West Blackhawk Street to sharpen their skills with rapiers, longswords, daggers, spears, and/or poleaxes. Many of them, along with their instructors, are members of the Chicago Swordplay Guild (CSG), founded in 1999 by Chicagoans Gregory Mele and Mark Rector.

The guild has more than eighty members ranging in age from their late teens to mid-fifties. Of these, fifty are active student members. Thirty percent are women. Class members typically wear workout clothes, but some of the students sport masks, metal throat armor (gorgets), and chest armor (gambesons).

The instructors are old-school. Really, really, really old-school. They base their lessons on documents written in the fifteenth and sixteenth centuries. Students learn not only how to hold and swing a sword, but how to stand and how to walk properly. Members of the guild who are particularly adventurous can learn how to engage in combat on horseback.

All of this goes to prove that unlike the age of chivalry, the art of European swordplay is not dead. Nor is it quite the same thing as what you see in movies like *Pirates of the Caribbean* or *Lord of the Rings*. For one thing, in films a sword fight often goes on and on, with the opponents banging their swords together using big gestures.

Leo Lastre and David Farrell get in the swing of things
during training at the Chicago Swordplay Guild.
©CHICAGO SWORDPLAY GUILD

A true swordfight is all about finding the quickest path to your opponent. The fight usually lasts about three seconds.

Playing with swords: It's not just for Sir Lancelot any more. Laissez-aller!

Main CSG classes are held in the Pulaski Park auditorium at 1419 West Blackhawk St. The CSG also offers classes in multiple city and suburban locations. For more information, send an e-mail to sword play@chicagoswordplayguild.com or visit www.chicagoswordplay guild.com/.

6

South Side
(including Southwest)

Hyde Park, one of the city's most famous neighborhoods, is located on the South Side. This area was the scene of the 1893 World's Columbian Exposition, and attractions include the Museum of Science and Industry, which is housed in the former Palace of Fine Arts.

Chinatown is located in the Armour Square community area, where you'll also find U.S. Cellular Field (formerly Comiskey Park), home of the Chicago White Sox baseball team.

Bronzeville, referred to as the "Black Metropolis" during the early twentieth century, is situated in the Douglas and Grand Boulevard community areas. Bronzeville is associated with many famous Americans, including Gwendolyn Brooks, Richard Wright, Louis Armstrong, and Bessie Coleman.

One of the most historic neighborhoods on the Southwest Side is Back of the Yards in New City. At one time it was home to vast numbers of immigrant laborers who worked at Union Stock Yards. Some of the neighborhoods on the Southwest Side, notably Englewood, are not recommended for tourists.

The Far Southwest Side offers an interesting mix of South Side and Irish culture. The community of Beverly is one of the city's few racially integrated neighborhoods. If you're looking for an authentic Irish pub, Mount Greenwood is your best bet.

Pullman on the Far Southeast Side has an intriguing history that revolves around George Pullman's attempt to build the "World's Most

Perfect Town" for his employees. The arts scene in South Shore is quite lively. Rainbow Beach is one of the city's best (and least known) beaches.

In Greater Grand you'll find Oak Woods Cemetery, the final resting place of "Big Jim" Colosimo, Enrico Fermi, Ida B. Wells, Jesse Owens— and 6,000 Confederate prisoners of war who died at Camp Douglas.

Also included in this chapter are curiosities located in Alsip and Justice.

Pump You Up!
Schaller's Pump

No, Schaller's Pump is not a gas station, nor is it an apparatus that draws water from a well. Schaller's Pump is a restaurant and bar that opened (under another name) in 1881. Located in the Bridgeport neighborhood, it's considered to be the oldest continuously operating tavern in the city of Chicago.

The "Pump" designation apparently dates back to Prohibition, when the two-story brick building on South Halsted housed a speak-easy. Beer was supposedly pumped straight into the place from the Ambrosia Brewery next door.

Those who would describe Schaller's Pump as a "hole in the wall" should ask to see the real hole in the wall—a peephole that allowed the speakeasy gatekeeper to screen people who knocked on the door. (Imagine being an employee, peering through that hole, and seeing federal agent Eliot Ness or one of his "Untouchables"!) To the left of the peephole is the buzzer that was pressed to permit entry.

These days Schaller's Pump is a great place to get pumped up for a White Sox game and to celebrate a win afterwards. A huge billboard on the outside wall proclaims WELCOME WHITE SOX FANS, and U.S. Cellular Field (formerly Comiskey Park) is within walking distance.

Naturally, Schaller's Pump has a back room. That's where Chicago politicians like former mayor Richard J. Daley, a son of the South Side, reportedly brokered many "deals." Apparently he wasn't concerned

**Kim Schaller reveals a peephole that dates from Pro-
hibition days in a door in Schaller's Pump.**

about the walls having ears. Neither were several other Chicago mayors who used Schaller's Pump as a "second office."

Baseball and politics: If that doesn't say "Chicago," I don't know
what does!

Schaller's Pump caters to anybody who appreciates Southside
Chicago accents, ice-cold beer, and a menu that features butt steak,
hash browns, burgers, and corned beef and cabbage. Bridgeport residents give Schaller's Pump high marks for food, decor (old tile floors,

★ ★

antique oak-back bar, wooden saloon-style cash register, neon Sox paraphernalia), and "southern" hospitality. It's also the place to go to hear fascinating stories about "the old days" from the people who lived them.

Schaller's Pump is located at 3714 South Halsted St. For more information, call (773) 376-6332.

Offensive on So Many Levels
The Vision Center Indian

Now, here's a "curiosity" that takes the idea of a cigar store Indian to new heights (or new lows, depending on your point of view).

Back in the 1800s a cigar store Indian's function was to identify a shop that sold tobacco. You see, Native Americans introduced tobacco to Europeans, so that made sense to people. I really don't know if anyone was offended by carved wooden Indians back then.

What we have on top of the Capital Cigar Store in the West Lawn community is another thing entirely. First of all, this guy is huge (probably around 17 feet high). Second, he's wearing a pair of glasses. Behind those glasses are bright white eyes that look like something out of a science fiction movie. He's wearing a sign that says EYE CAN SEE NOW. (This is presumably because an eye clinic is located beneath his feet, in the same building as the cigar store.)

Our fine fellow is known by various names, including the

Trivia

The world-famous Harlem Globetrotters got their start in Chicago in 1926 as the "Savoy Big 5," coached by Abe Saperstein. They became the Harlem Globetrotters in 1927.

★ ★

"Vision Center Indian," "Eye Care Indian," "63rd Street Indian," and "Cigar Store Indian." He is also occasionally called, "What-the-heck-is-that-are-you-kidding-me?"

It's hard to know where to start. We can probably safely assume that a fair number of Native Americans would be offended by this

Is the Vision Center Indian a sight for sore eyes—or just an eyesore?

monstrosity. But think of the other groups who might object: people who wear glasses, for example, or people with white eyes. Or non-smokers (it is, after all, a cigar store Indian). I could go on, but I don't want to make the big guy angry. I've been told I wouldn't like him when he's angry.

The Vision Center Indian resides at 6258 South Pulaski Rd.

It's All about YOU!
Museum of Science and Industry

Don't you hate it when you try to express how you feel about something and somebody says, "Hey, it's not always about you!" You'll be happy to know that the folks at the Museum of Science and Industry sympathize. I'm sure that's why they titled their new permanent exhibit "YOU! The Experience." It really is all about you. And me. Actually, it's about all human beings. But that's okay, right?

It's also about Stan the Man. No, not Stan "The Man" Musial, for those of you old enough to know who that is. In this case "Stan" isn't short for "Stanley"; it's short for "Stan D. Ardman" (or "Standard Man"—get it?). Stan is a Human Patient Simulator—the first to be displayed in any museum. To put it in simpler terms, he's a computer-controlled mannequin. (I could therefore call him "Stan the MANN-equin," but I won't. You're welcome.)

Stan can breathe, blink, and simulate real medical conditions—he can even talk. He's normally used for training at medical and nursing schools. Visitors to the Museum of Science and Industry get to use this technology to learn how to diagnose and treat ailments such as asthma and obesity-induced diabetes. I suppose this is a good thing, although a little knowledge can be dangerous. Hopefully the exhibit doesn't inspire anyone to try practicing medicine without a license. Most of the people I saw there weren't even in their teens yet.

In addition to playing doctor with Stan, you can watch blood pulsing through your veins, run on a human-size hamster wheel, get a sneak peek at what you'll look like in twenty years, and stare in

★ ★

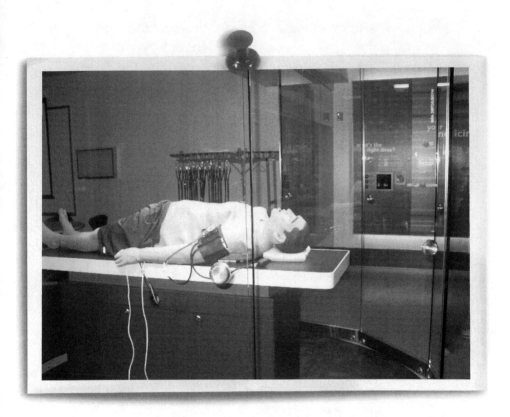

Visitors to the Museum of Science and Industry get to
"play doctor" with Stan.

amazement at a 13-foot-tall replica of a human heart that beats in
time with your heartbeat. You'll also want to check out the multi-
media presentation on the development of a human fetus and a
bunch of other exhibits that are all about YOU.

Completely unrelated to Stan but worth noting is the fact that the
Museum of Science and Industry is the only building that remains
from the 1893 World's Columbian Exhibition. It's located at 57th
Street and Lake Shore Drive. For more information, call (773) 684-
1414 or visit www.msichicago.org.

Where's the Pool?

The Capone House

Based on what we see on television and in movies, the homes of big crime bosses are sprawling estates with million-dollar furnishings and massive swimming pools. That's why it's such a surprise when you pull up in front of the two-story red brick duplex on South Prairie Avenue on Chicago's far South Side.

Al Capone controlled the Chicago underworld in the 1920s from this modest brick house.

155

★ ★

From 1923 to 1931 this modest house was occupied by a man, his wife, his mother, his children, and other relatives. The thing is, the man wasn't just any man. He was Al Capone, America's best-known gangster.

From this four-bedroom, two-bath house built in 1908, Capone controlled the Chicago underworld while telling neighbors he was in the furniture business. The balcony on the second floor has a great view of Chicago. The basement windows have bars on them. Out back, Capone built a brick garage for his armor-plated Cadillac.

In April 1924 the home was the location of an elaborate gangland funeral for Capone's brother Frank, killed by police in a gunfight. In the kitchen, from time to time, Capone would cook spaghetti for reporters, an apron tied around his waist and bedroom slippers on his feet. In December 1927 Capone was virtually a prisoner in the house when it was surrounded by police who threatened to arrest anyone who left or entered.

The family sold the house in 1953 when Capone's mother died. By then Capone himself had been dead for six years. He died at his home in Miami Beach, a two-story wood-sided home with ten rooms and—yes—a swimming pool.

The Chicago house was nominated for consideration as a historic landmark in 1989, but opponents objected on the grounds that such an act would honor a vicious criminal, revive Chicago's gangland past, and perpetuate the stereotyping of all Italian Americans. The nomination was withdrawn.

The Capone house is located at 7244 South Prairie Ave. It is not open to the public.

Humanity's Best and Worst
Douglas Tomb/Camp Douglas

They called him "The Little Giant." Short in physical stature but enormously influential and successful in politics, Illinois native Stephen A. Douglas played a key role in Chicago's development. His

A monument and row of gravestones mark the largest
Northern burial site for Confederate soldiers.

accomplishments were many and varied, but he's often remembered
as Abraham Lincoln's opponent in the famed Lincoln-Douglas debates
of 1858.

Douglas spent the last years of his life at Oakenwald, his fifty-
three-acre estate just east of the present-day intersection of Cottage
Grove Avenue and 35th Street. After his death in 1861, the U.S. gov-
ernment constructed a training camp for Union soldiers on the property. Camp Douglas, as it was called, also became a prisoner-of-war
compound.

Overcrowding, disease, cruel punishments, arctic temperatures, and

★ ★

starvation killed more than 6,000 Confederate soldiers between February 1862, when the camp received its first prisoners, and the summer of 1865, when it closed.

Douglas is buried on the site where Oakenwald and Camp Douglas once stood. A 96-foot-tall granite structure commemorates the Little Giant's remarkable life. The grounds surrounding the tomb are landscaped with numerous trees and flower beds.

About 5 miles south, in Oak Woods Cemetery, a monument erected by Southern veterans marks the location of the remains of Confederate prisoners who died at Camp Douglas. According to a plaque at the site, "The bronze statue surmounting the battlemented cap of the column is a realistic representation of a Confederate

How . . . Awkward

The date was April 21, 1986. The setting was "Scarface" Al Capone's former headquarters at the Lexington Hotel at South Michigan Avenue. On live national television, reporter Geraldo Rivera prepared to dynamite a concrete vault. What would he find inside? Money? Skeletons?

A medical examiner was standing by, as was an IRS agent (Capone, though dead for nearly forty years, still owed back taxes). Years of waiting and wondering were about to end!

And end they did. The vault contained a few empty bottles, an old sign, and dirt. Lots of dirt.

Rivera's career wasn't the first ruined by Al Capone, but it might have been the last.

infantry soldier after the surrender. The face expresses sorrow for the thousands of prison dead interred beneath."

The Douglas Tomb is located at 636 East 35th St. For more information, call (312) 225-2620 or visit www.state.il.us/hpa/hs/douglas _tomb.html. Oak Woods Cemetery is located at 1035 East 67th St. (67th Street and Cottage Grove). For more information, call (773) 288-3800.

The Mojo Is Gone
Garden of Sacred Hymns

The pipe organ is what you notice first. At least it looks like a pipe organ, sitting right there in the middle of that broad expanse of grass. But the sign over the gate says RESTVALE. This is a cemetery. Who would leave a pipe organ in a cemetery? On closer inspection, you see that the gold coloring is flaking off the pipes, which are attached to a monument made of rock, not a musical instrument. The sign on the monument reads GARDEN OF SACRED HYMNS.

But if there were to be a working pipe organ in any cemetery, it might just be this one. Restvale Cemetery contains the graves of some of America's best-known and best-loved blues musicians.

I'm talking about people like guitarist Samuel "Magic Sam" Maghett (1936–1969), piano player Clarence "Pine Top" Smith (1904–1929), and guitarist, mandolin player, and songwriter Charles "Papa Charlie" McCoy (1909–1950). A walk through Restvale is a walk through the world of blues legends.

If you could gather them all around that organ for a jam session, you'd have guitarist and singer John Henry Barbee (1905–1964), guitarist Earl Zebedee Hooker (1929–1970), and Walter "Shakey" Horton (1918–1981), aka King of the Blues Harmonica. And let's not forget McKinley Morganfield (1915–1983) on harmonica and guitar. You might know him as Muddy Waters. His gravestone reads THE MOJO IS GONE. THE MASTER HAS WON.

If anyone could play this pipe organ, it would be some
of the blues legends buried in this cemetery.

On a quiet evening, along about dusk, if you listen closely you
might hear a blues riff that'll send chills up your spine. Their music
lives on, even if the pipe organ that shares their final resting place
never sounds a note.

Restvale Cemetery is located at 11700 South Laramie Ave., in Alsip.
For more information, call (708) 385-3506.

The Golden Lady

Statue of the Republic

Your multiple-choice question is: What is that immense statue standing in the Hayes-Richards Circle in Jackson Park? Is it (a) Goldfinger's greatest achievement, (b) the Oscar for Most Colossal Actor or Actress

The Golden Lady is plenty big, but she used to be even bigger.

★ ★

Starring in a Motion Picture, (c) the last person King Midas ever touched, or (d) none of the above.

Well, that didn't take you long, did it? Of course it's (d) none of the above. The gilded bronze sculpture at the intersection of 63rd Street and Hayes Drive is a scaled-down replica of Daniel Chester French's *Statue of the Republic.* The original, created for the World's Columbian Exposition of 1893, stood 65 feet tall (more than 100 feet tall including the base).

Any resemblance between the Republic and the Statue of Liberty in New York was purely . . . intentional. Visitors to the fair could see the gigantic, shiny lady quite a distance away from her location at the eastern end of the Court of Honor, where she shared the stage with the Grand Basin (a large reflecting pool) and the elaborate Columbian Fountain by Frederick MacMonnies.

The original statue succumbed to fire in 1896. In 1918 Daniel Chester French was commissioned to create a 24-foot version of the statue (one third the size of the original) in honor of the twenty-fifth anniversary of the fair and the centennial of Illinois's statehood. The base of the replica was created by Henry Bacon, French's collaborator on the later Lincoln Memorial in Washington, D.C.

The replica differs from the original statue in more ways than size. In both, the woman's right hand holds a globe with an eagle perched or hovering on top. (The globe and eagle were the fair's emblem.) However, in the original the left hand held a lance decorated with laurel leaves and a Phrygian cap representing the French Revolution. The replica holds a staff with a laurel wreath in its left hand.

The statue was re-gilded in 1992 for the hundredth anniversary of the exposition, and was designated a Chicago Landmark in 2003. It's located at 63rd Street and Hayes Drive in Jackson Park.

Name Withheld to Protect the Foolish

A *Tribune* reporter writing in August 1865 thoughtfully withheld the name of his subject, a man who lived on Cottage Grove Avenue. The man had returned home from a trip late at night, a day earlier than expected. After crawling under the covers with his wife, he heard heavy breathing beneath the bed. At first he feared it was a burglar. Next he imagined that his wife had a lover who had gone into hiding. The man drew his pistol and fired beneath the bed. A blood-curdling howl told him he had shot his own dog. "Over the ensuing scene," the reporter wrote, "let us mercifully draw the veil."

Duryea Takes the Prize!
America's First Automobile Race

The day of the Big Race—November 28, 1895—dawned cold and windy. Twelve inches of snow lay on the ground, covered by a frozen crust. This would not have been a problem had the participants been using dogsleds. However, this wasn't the Iditarod. This race, from the World's Fair German Building in Jackson Park to Evanston and back, was to be America's first horseless carriage race.

Out of a field of more than sixty entrants, only eleven agreed to participate under the less-than-ideal conditions. Five broke down on their way to the starting point. The six who remained battled knee-deep icy slush, disastrous encounters with horse-drawn carriages, and boys throwing snowballs. In the end, a gasoline-powered vehicle

★ ★

made by the Duryea Wagon Motor Company of Springfield, Massachusetts, was the winner.

According to umpire Arthur White, the Duryea machine covered 54.36 miles in 7 hours and 53 minutes, averaging a little more than 7 miles per hour.

You can visit a plaque commemorating the race in Jackson Park between 59th and 60th Streets, just west of Cornell Drive, near the Perennial Garden.

German Soldier Met His Waterloo in Chicago
The Von Zirngibl Grave

Born in Russia in 1797, Andreas Von Zirngibl fought Napoleon at Waterloo under General Gebhard von Blucher. Von Zirngibl literally "gave his right arm" for the cause.

Von Zirngibl paid for this land and, by golly, he intends to stay here!

★ ★

After the war, Von Zirngibl married and took up fishing in Germany. He and his wife had five children. In the 1850s he moved his family to America. Arriving in Chicago in 1853, he purchased forty-four acres of land near the mouth of the Calumet River. The fishing was good there, and Von Zirngibl loved his new home. Unfortunately, he died of a fever in 1855.

The German veteran's last request was to be buried on the land for which he had paid $160 in gold. His sons honored that request.

Von Zirngibl's grave remains at its original location, in spite of the fact that the area is now a scrap yard. Over the years, attempts to move the burial site have been stopped by court decisions. It was rededicated in 1987 and serves as a reminder of all the immigrants who came to America in search of a better life.

The Von Zirngibl grave resides at 9331 South Ewing Ave.

Lincoln's Englewood Address
The Wolcott Avenue Bust

If you know anything about Illinois, you know that statues and busts of Abraham Lincoln are plentiful throughout the state. In Chicago, these can be found in places like Lincoln Park, Garfield Park, Senn Park, Lincoln Square, Grant Park . . . not to mention the corner of South Wolcott Avenue and 69th Street. I say "not to mention" because you won't find this particular homage to the Great Emancipator mentioned in guidebooks.

It's a 5-foot-tall bust of Lincoln that has been sitting in front of the Lincoln Gas Station in Englewood since 1926.

When photographer and sociologist Camilo José Vergara first took note of the bust in 1997, it had been painted black. A year later, Vergara reports, the statue was white. By 2004 it was dappled "like a Dalmatian." Vergara stopped by again in 2007 and discovered that the bust had been repainted, and a well-known Chicago gang had drawn their symbol on it.

In the fall of 2009, when I paid a visit to this unsung tribute to

★ ★

Honest Abe, it was basically white but weather-beaten, its coat of paint chipped and flaking. Its nose was broken off. I don't know when, why, or how that happened.

The statue's eyes are still there, though. Imagine the sights and scenes that have taken place on that spot during more than eighty years of sentry duty.

Vergara's photographs of the bust over the years can be found at www.slate.com/id/2210561.

Every neighborhood in Illinois should have a
5-foot-tall Lincoln bust on the corner!

Chicago Nerd Social Club

As the poet Percy B. Shelley wrote in 1820: "Hail to thee, blithe Spirit! Nerd thou never wert." Oh wait. That's *bird* thou never wert, not nerd. How do I know this? Because I'm a poetry nerd!

There are many types of nerds (people who are extremely interested in and knowledgeable about a particular subject). You might think that a nerd, by definition, is unsociable. You would be wrong. In Chicago in 2009, nerds Rachel Baker, Scott Newberger, and Jeff Smith formed the Chicago Nerd Social Club (CNSC).

What sort of events does a nerd social club sponsor? How about a Halloween party featuring Nerd O'Lanterns (pumpkins with a bit of geeky flair)? Or a Pi Day event, where attendees bring pies and participate in a Pi Off to see who can recall pi to the most decimal points? Other events have included a Beer Expedition (to explore eight beers rarely seen in North American bars), a Video Game LAN Party, and a Techie Nerds Karaoke Night.

The organization has also sponsored seminars and classes such as Comic Book Academia, Dungeons and Dragons 101, Effective Interviewing, and a Robot Work Shop.

For more information about the CNSC, visit www.chicagonerds.com.

Chicago's Gateway Arch
Union Stock Yards Entrance

Union Stock Yards was big. Known simply as "The Yards," it sprawled over 475 acres. Tens of thousands of people worked at the Yards, and millions of animals were processed there. The grounds contained hotels, saloons, restaurants, offices, and more than 2,000 livestock pens. From the Civil War until the 1920s, Chicago was America's largest meatpacking center.

In addition to being big, Union Stock Yards was bad and ugly. If you don't believe me, read Upton Sinclair's book *The Jungle.* The book describes the sights, smells, and sounds of the stockyards in horrifying, graphic detail. Sinclair later noted: "I aimed at the public's heart, and by accident I hit it in the stomach." Yes, Upton, yes you did.

Those who spent any time near the stockyards didn't need Sinclair to make them feel sick. They inhaled the ghastly odors and listened to screaming animals day in and day out.

One of the few visual reminders of this era in Chicago history still stands on Exchange Avenue. It's big, but certainly not bad or ugly (at least not in my opinion). It's a limestone gateway designed by the architectural firm of Burnham and Root in 1875. It isn't as splendiferous as the Gateway Arch in Saint Louis, but it holds a significant place in history.

John B. Sherman—the founder of the Union Stock Yard & Transit Company—commissioned the work. It's thought that the limestone steer head over the central arch represents "Sherman," a prize-winning bull named after founder Sherman (who also happened to be architect Daniel Burnham's father-in law).

The Yards closed in 1971 after several decades of decline. Designated a Chicago Landmark a year later, the stockyards arch became a National Historic Landmark in 1981.

Today the area is an industrial park. On the other side of the rugged yet dignified gateway is a monument dedicated to twenty-one firemen who perished during a fire at Union Stock Yards in 1910. The monument's base contains the names of all Chicago firefighters who have died in the line of duty.

The Union Stock Yards Gate and Fire Memorial are located at South Peoria Street and West Exchange Avenue. For more information, visit http://egov.cityofchicago.org/Landmarks/index.html.

Sherman the bull gazes out from the Union Stock Yards entrance gate.

Trivia

In spite of its inhospitable winters, Chicago boasts a colony of wild tropical birds whose bright green and blue plumage can be seen in the treetops of Hyde Park. These monk parakeets (*Myiopsitta monachus*) make their presence known by enthusiastically chirping and screeching. No one knows exactly how they ended up in Chicago.

★ ★

Chicago's Most Famous Ghost

Resurrection Mary

A blonde, blue-eyed girl in a white dress darts in front of cars late at night on Archer Avenue, forcing motorists to slam on their brakes. Sometimes she vanishes immediately. Other times, she crumples to the ground, then disappears before the driver can get out of the car. On still other occasions, the automobile passes right through her.

Picked up as a hitchhiker or offered a ride home by someone she meets at a dance hall, she disappears when the car reaches Resurrection Cemetery in Justice, a few miles southwest of Chicago. She is known throughout the region—and even the nation—as "Resurrection Mary."

Legend has it that a girl named Mary was killed by a hit-and-run driver as she was walking up Archer Avenue one night. Her parents buried her in Resurrection Cemetery in the white dancing dress she was wearing when she died.

Who is Resurrection Mary? Is she Anna "Marija" Norkus, who died in a 1927 automobile accident on the way home from the Oh Henry Ballroom? Or is she Mary Bregovy, who died in a 1934 automobile accident in the Loop?

Reports of encounters with this lovely ghost began in the 1930s and continue to the present day. For more information, visit www.chicagohauntings.com or www.ghostsofchicago.com.

index

index

index

index

index

175

index

index

⭑ ⭑

index

about the author

Scotti McAuliff Cohn grew up in Springfield, Illinois, and has many fond memories of visiting family and friends in Chicago over the years. Today she lives in Bloomington, Illinois, where she works as a freelance writer and copy editor. Her other books for Globe Pequot Press include *It Happened in Chicago* and *Illinois: Mapping the Prairie State through History*. Scotti maintains a website at www.scotticohn.com. She also writes a blog at http://ihichicago.blogspot.com that features information about her books and interviews with other writers who have Chicago connections.